T. C. (Theophilus Charles) Noble

A Brief History of the Worshipful Company of Ironmongers

London, A. D. 1351-1889

T. C. (Theophilus Charles) Noble

A Brief History of the Worshipful Company of Ironmongers
London, A. D. 1351-1889

ISBN/EAN: 9783337180935

Printed in Europe, USA, Canada, Australia, Japan

Cover: Foto ©ninafisch / pixelio.de

More available books at **www.hansebooks.com**

Arms of the Worshipful Company of Ironmongers.

(See page 14.)

A BRIEF HISTORY

OF

THE WORSHIPFUL COMPANY OF IRONMONGERS

LONDON

A.D. 1351-1889

WITH

AN APPENDIX CONTAINING SOME ACCOUNT OF THE BLACKSMITHS' COMPANY

BY

T. C. NOBLE

WARDEN OF THE YEOMANRY OF THE IRONMONGERS' COMPANY

1888-1889

WITH NUMEROUS ILLUSTRATIONS BY GEORGE CRUIKSHANK AND OTHERS

London

PRINTED FOR PRIVATE CIRCULATION ONLY

MARCH 1889

PREFACE.

To my brother Ironmongers, "root and branch," I dedicate this "brief history" of our ancient Guild. Notwithstanding the innumerable facts printed in the following pages, the work must only be considered as an historical essay upon the tenth of the twelve "great" Livery Companies of the City of London. A more elaborate compilation is in progress, and if my life is spared to complete it that work will contain the labour of love collections during the past quarter of a century of an extensive—I may say unique—assortment of manuscripts and other papers relating to the City, its Companies, and its Institutions, which will prove, I have every reason to believe, a most interesting and valuable civic record.

The present publication has taken place now for several reasons, some of which I may as well explain. Before J. P. Malcolm printed the interesting extracts from the Ironmongers' records in the second volume of his "Londinium Redivivum," 1803, very little was known by the general public about this ancient City Guild. He was followed by William Herbert, the Guildhall Librarian, in 1834-36, who published a "History of the Twelve Great Livery Companies," with a most valuable introductory essay. Both of these works are now scarce. In 1851 John Nicholl, Esq., F.S.A., a Member of the Court of the Ironmongers' Company, compiled his "Some Account" of the Guild, taken from their own records, and this choice volume he enlarged and printed in 1866. There were, however, only 150 copies circulated among the Livery and their friends, consequently this history is more scarce than those issued by Malcolm and Herbert.

When I was elected Yeomanry Warden at Easter, 1888, in commemoration of the fact that I was one of the Committee of the Spanish Armada Tercentenary (Plymouth and London) Commemoration, about which Armada I had published an essay in 1886, and that the Ironmongers' Company had contributed towards the defence of the kingdom exactly three centuries previous; that the year 1889 was by a curious coincidence the 700th anniversary of the City Mayoralty; that several eminent Lord Mayors had been citizens and Ironmongers; that from my own personal knowledge a large percentage of the present members of the Yeomanry know very little of the history of their Guild, or about their ancient predecessors; and last, but not least, that the facilities afforded to me by the Editor of the well-known trade journal, THE IRONMONGER, for the publication in its columns during the past three months of this "brief history," which has had a circulation not second to any other weekly throughout the world, prompted me to forward a long-cherished project of compiling for my brethren a short history, and thus commemorate their kindness for electing me their representative. The unexpected opportunity of holding a most enthusiastic meeting on St. Luke's Day, 1888, at the London Tavern, opposite Ironmongers' Hall (our Hall being temporarily closed), enabled me, as their Warden, to give to my brother Ironmongers the first historical discourse relating to the Company (see Chapter VI.), and it helped to comfort their disappointment in being unable to meet in their own Hall upon the anniversary of the day they had assembled therein for nearly three hundred years.

Then, again, there are some personal reasons worth mentioning. A citizen born, the great-grandson of an eighteenth-century engineer and ironfounder, the grandson of a ship-owner, newspaper proprietor, and possessor of the historical property in the district which he named King's Cross, and where to this day several of the great "iron roads" of England meet, and the son of a publisher and bookseller of Fleet Street, whose memory and that of my birthplace I commemorated in 1869 in the "Memorials" of the neighbourhood—in which year, too, by another remarkable coincidence, I was honoured by being admitted a member of the Ironmongers' Company without the payment of fees—an honour only conferred on those who perform their duty to their fellow-citizens.

When the then member for Cork City asked Parliament twenty years ago to seize the estates of the Companies in Ireland, I was fortunately enabled by my knowledge of the subject to assist in the defeat of this wild, revolutionary scheme of seizing property personally paid for by the ancestors of the citizens of London. It was the Hon. the Irish Society and the Companies who voted me their thanks, and it was my two ever-revered friends, John Nicholl, our historian, and S. Adams Beck, our then clerk (the father of our present zealous official)—the memory of whom will long remain dear, for their portraits hang side by side in our Court-room—it was their kind notice of my humble efforts, and their repeated good advice, which helped me to the honour I so highly valued, and led me to be ever watchful of our rights and privileges.

Thirty years ago my said dear friend John Nicholl was Master of the Company (he died in 1871), and this year his son is our Senior Warden, and (I trust) our next Master. We wish him every best wish, we heartily pray that the Almighty will bless us all, and that "the Worshipful Company of Ironmongers, root and branch," may be permitted to "flourish for ever."

Dalston,
London,
March, 1889.

T. C. NOBLE,
Warden of the Yeomanry,
1888–1889.

CONTENTS.

APPENDIX.

ILLUSTRATIONS.

The Old Church of Allhallows Staining, Mark Lane, London, 1807. (See page 45.)

The Church of St. Luke the Evangelist, Old Street, Middlesex, 1807. (See page 57.)

A BRIEF HISTORY

OF THE

IRONMONGERS' COMPANY.

CHAPTER I.

THE OLD CITY, ITS CITIZENS AND GUILDS.

IN the history of the ancient Livery Companies of London we read the history and progress of not only the City but the Empire. During the many centuries of their existence the Guilds have performed a work for which they deserve the praise and continued support of not only every citizen, but every man who to-day enjoys the freedom of local self-government. There have been kings and prime ministers who, in their tyrannical measures, have forgotten the interests of the people and their trades in their desire to gain unlawful ends, but in every case for hundreds of years the citizens and the Guilds of London have stood forward to fight the great battles for freedom, and the continued and present existence of the Corporation of the ancient City, and the good work they do to-day, prove, if we carefully read their history, that to them we are more deeply indebted than "reformers" choose to acknowledge.

Generations ago "the City" was a very small place, surrounded by a wall with gates, through which the green fields and suburbs—then the pleasant villages of Southwark, Charing, St. Giles, Clerkenwell, Islington, Shoreditch, and the Tower Hamlets and Stepney—could be reached. These gates stood at or near the entrances of the present streets known as Moorgate, Cripplegate, Aldersgate, Newgate, Ludgate, Billingsgate, Aldgate, and Bishopsgate, so that the reader can judge what the size of old London was. On the south side there was the River Thames with its Dowgate, and between this water-gate and Billingsgate was the entrance across the only bridge that then spanned the river, which existed close to where St. Magnus Church now stands—a few yards east of the present London Bridge. In the suburbs were many excellent springs of water, known as Holywells, and at one of these the parish clerks of the City assembled periodically and held their festivals. The well existed till late years in Ray Street, close to the Middlesex Sessions House, and the district is now known as Clerkenwell. The Parish Clerks' Company, although not a livery guild, still exists, and is one of the oldest of the Guilds.

It was long before the time of famous John Stow that London found a contemporary topographer, for as early as the year 1179—now 710 years ago—William Fitzstephen tells us the citizens everywhere "are esteemed the politest of all others in their manners, their dress, and the elegance and splendour of their tables," and he pictures us the City in all its primitive grandeur, while the citizens themselves were dignified by the name of barons, a fact borne out by their description in King John's charter. Speaking of this charter reminds us that a brief epitome of the principal grants, from the Conquest to the reign of Edward IV., when the Ironmongers' Company received its incorporation, will help the reader to more easily comprehend the progress of the citizens and the Guilds.

There is no document more treasured at Guildhall than the diminutive parchment which William the Conqueror gave to the citizens 800 years ago, and upon which we all base our rights and privileges.

> I will that ye be worthy
> of all those laws which
> ye were in King Edward's day:
> and I will that each child
> be his father's heir after his
> father's day, and I will not
> suffer that any man do you
> wrong. God preserve you.

In the Confessor's time "the burgesses" of London had obtained the king's warrant for their freedom, and their children's heirship, so that their lives and their goods should be protected from the rapacity of the Lords. The foreign merchant was only permitted in the City as a lodger, and was strictly forbidden from selling his wares by retail and underselling and infringing the rights of his entertainer, the citizen. Thus do we see nearly a thousand years ago a precaution taken which we to-day are still clamouring for!

King Henry I., for a quit rent of 300*l.* per annum, granted the citizens the Sheriffwick of Middlesex, which 750 years later has been taken from them. The same monarch also granted them the privilege of hunting, and it is probably through this right the Londoners obtained of late years, for ever, Epping Forest as an open space.

Being dependent upon the king, before the days of charter rights the citizens were often sorely fleeced upon the slightest pretence, and in order to protect themselves they in process of time formed guilds or fraternities of different trades. Richard I. freed them from toll and lestage throughout England, and gave them the conservancy of the River Thames, which right was taken from them some thirty years ago. Of course King John enlarged their privileges in 1199, for the City paid him 3,000 marks, and kings would do anything if you paid them handsomely. Five charters out of eight granted by Henry III. cost them one-fifteenth of their estate, and for another, dated 1265, they paid 13,000*l.* We mention this to show that having bought these privileges it is unreasonable to deprive them of their rights without compensation, and yet this question is never properly understood or thought of.

In the fifth charter granted by King John (1214) the citizens of London received the privilege of choosing their own Mayor from among themselves, and it is to this right many of the livery companies owe their foundation. The first Edward permitted the Chief Magistrate to be sworn in before the Constable at the Tower should the king or his judges be absent from London; and, furthermore, no stranger was to be admitted to the City freedom unless six honest and sufficient members of a mystery or trade be surety. In 1311 Edward II. exempted the citizens from service outside the City in the time of war or tumult, and for this privilege the king was favoured with a gift of 2,000 marks.

To King Edward III. the citizens are indebted for many of their most valued privileges. Thus, in 1327, the Mayor was instituted one of the judges in trials at the Old Bailey (Newgate), the right to bring felons from any part of England and to their goods, the right of devising in Mortmain and forbidding the holding of markets within seven miles of the City. And in order to give them control over such persons as escaped to Southwark to avoid justice, that ancient village was added to the City liberties (and subsequently designated Bridge Ward Without). In 1337 the same king confirmed the rights and privileges, forbidding "foreign" merchant traders retailing in the City and acting as brokers; and in 1354 granted a fifth charter, permitting the Mayor to have gold or silver maces carried before him, from which time the title of Lord Mayor of London has been assumed by London's Chief Magistrate.

Edward IV. was not behind his predecessors in favouring the citizens, but then it must be noted they paid him some 12,000*l.* for four charters. In 1462 the Mayor, ex-Mayors, and Recorder were all made perpetual justices, and were exempted from serving on juries, &c., while Bartholomew Fair, with a court of Pie Poudre, was to be held in Smithfield. And in 1478 they obtained the right of electing a coroner, and for wine-gauging, &c. As it was Edward IV. who granted the Ironmongers their charter, we have traced the progress of the City privileges so far, and leave the Ironmongers' records to tell the tale of subsequent progress.

In the course of the preceding remarks the citizens have been so continually alluded to, that a few notes about them and what really constituted a citizen will not be out of place here. In the first place, we think it is not generally known that every member of a City Company is a citizen of London, but every citizen is not a member of a Company. There are two grades of citizens—one free of the City only; the other free of both City and Company, the latter freeman being designated as "citizen and ironmonger," or whatever Company he may belong to. As the elections or admissions to all the Companies are the same, that describing the admission to the Ironmongers' will be found in a subsequent chapter of our history.

In all the early charters the general term is "citizens," but the Conqueror calls them "burhwarn" (inhabitants or burgesses of the borough), and John and Henry III. call them "barons." The citizens or freemen were the men or inhabitants of free condition and householders, in contradistinction to the bondsmen or villains of the great lords. In the time of Henry III. (1260) all persons of the age of twelve years and upwards were commanded to swear allegiance to the king. In 1305 four persons who held land from the Bishop of London, and dwelt outside the City, were deprived of their freedom, and about the same time the City records declare that everyone who is sworn a freeman, and acts contrary to his oath, should be compelled to "forsweare the town" and lose his privileges. The statute of the 18th

Edward II. for View of Frankpledge contains a list of articles still in use, but the statute has been improperly neglected. In 1326 all alien merchants were directed to be amerced, and in 1364 it was ordained that a citizen should obtain his privileges by birth (as a son of a citizen), by servitude (as an apprentice), or by presentment of a mystery or Guild. In 1377, and for a few years after, it was decreed that members of the Common Council should only be chosen from the mysteries, and in 1385 a most important decision was come to, for upon the complaint of the Mercers and the Drapers that some persons had been improperly admitted to the Haberdashers' and Weavers' Guilds who were not of those trades, they were at once expelled the City. In the seventh year of Edward IV. no freeman or officer of the City was to be allowed to use the livery of any lord or great man, on pain of losing his office and freedom, so it is pretty evident the two evils which at the present time (1889) beset us—foreign traders and civil servant traders—were not unknown 400 years ago.

We shall conclude this the first chapter of our history by a brief notice of what is to be understood by the description "Guild." In ancient times Guilds or Gilds were of two kinds—religious and secular. The term "Guilds" is from the Saxon—to pay, an amerciement or payment towards the support of a brotherhood. The religious Guilds existed until their dissolution by Edward VI.; their foundations in some cases were very early, for at Glemsford, in Suffolk, in Canute's time, existed a fraternity of clerks. In London, the "Cnughts" or "Cnighten Gild," of thirteen persons, had their district or soke outside the City walls, near the Tower, and was the origin of Portsoken Ward. The Gilda Theutonicorum,* the steel-yard merchants of Dowgate, who first existed 900 years ago, and held a most important position, had their guildhall in the neighbourhood where of late years the iron trade has been so well known (Thames Street), and yet it must be borne in mind that the definition of *steel-yard* was in reality a yard for warehousing general *staple* goods, and not solely for steel or iron ware. The transfer of all trade concerns to the management and jurisdiction of the Craft Guild was generally accomplished by a confirmation of their ordinance, that everyone carrying on a trade within the town should join the Guild, for which the Guild paid certain taxes—in London to the King—and under Henry I. (1100-1133), and every succeeding reign, the Weavers paid a fee-farm rent, and in 1179 no less than eighteen Guilds were amerced as adulterine, or set up without licence. This was the same year that Fitzstephen tells us the followers of the several trades, the vendors of various commodities, and the labourers of every kind were to be found in their proper and distinct places. Now, in proof of this, we find that to this day in the neighbourhood of Cheap (market) side the streets and lanes still exist wherein the particular trades in the old City were carried on, viz., Milk Street, Bread Street Poultry, Cornhill, Wood Street, Candlewick (now Cannon, Street, and Ironmonger Lane—in which latter thoroughfare and Old Jewry, close to the Guildhall, the ironmongers of old London carried on their business, as will be proved in another chapter.

Many of the ancient Guilds in local places which related to ironmongers will be mentioned further on, but we may mention that Walford, speaking of the Reading Cutlers' and Bellfounders' Guilds, tells us that one of their orders was:—

"No smith may sell iron wares within the borough except a freeman, on forfeiture of two shillings each time." Next to the Saddlers' and Weavers' Guilds of London in antiquity are the Glovers' and the Blacksmiths'—the latter ordinances are dated 1434—and of this particular Company the writer of the present history will at some future time give some interesting and little known details. Suffice it to say now that one of the orders particularly ordained: "If eny of the seid bretheren or there wyves be absent fro oure comon dyner or elles fro oure quater dai schall paie as moche as if he or sho ware present." It is proved in this ordinance that dinners were common with the City Guilds four centuries ago, and that the wives of the members were of as much importance to the craft as the members themselves. At the present day, we regret to find that the ladies are not always considered with so brotherly an attention as the blacksmiths considered their ladies in King Henry's day.

Another of the ancient Guilds was the Farriers', whose orders, about the year 1324, included the charges to be made for shoeing horses, at the rate of a penny halfpenny for six nails, and twopence for eight nails.

In Buckingham there was a Guild called the Mercers', which existed from early days. Even as late as the seventeenth century the minutes of this Company contained many very curious entries. For instance, in 1665, when Thomas Arnott, the eldest son of Walter Arnott, was made free upon the understanding that he was "to follow the trade of an ironmonger," he paid "one gallon of good wyne for his freedom," and when his brother Thomas was admitted in 1671 "to follow only ye trade of an ironmonger," he also paid the like fee. Upon turning to the ordinances of the Company we find that the ironmongers of the borough were, with other trades, associated under the name of the Mercers', and that the fifth clause particularly orders "noe strange pson or fforeigner inhabiting within the said borough or pish, and not ffree of the same, shall bee made ffree of the said Companies to the intent to sell or utter any kind of wares usually solde by any artificier, before such time as every such strange or forrein pson have paid for his freedome"—the sums specified in a schedule annexed, and which "for every ironmonger" was 20*l*., and "one good leather buckett for the use of the said Corporation," and that the son of such person or freeman so admitted shall, upon being made free of the Company "whereunto he hath beene an apprentice in forme aforesaid," pay to "the bayliffe and burgesses and his Company one gallon of good wyne."

As we proceed with our history we shall find some curious facts connected with the London ironmongers, and that their ordinances, quaint and still in force, contain many very illustrative evidences of the trade-unions of centuries ago.

CHAPTER II.

IRON, IRONWORKS, AND IRONMONGERS.

IRON and its uses historically described should form no unimportant part to the history of the Ironmongers' Company, but as it is not our intention now to give the thousand-and-one notes which would form a most interesting and valuable compendium to the general account of the City Guild, it is sufficient for us if we so condense our large store of material and give such an epitome as will assist the reader to comprehend the origin of the trade of which the company bears the name.

A well-known writer justly observes that no one should fail to consider the origin, history, and value of iron; that our instruments of cutlery, the tools of our mechanics, and the countless machines which we construct by the infinitely varied applications of iron are derived from ore for the most part coeval with or more ancient than the fuel by the aid of which we reduce it to its metallic state, and apply it to innumerable uses in the economy of human life. The use of iron is identified with the time of erecting the Egyptian monuments, the oldest in the world, and a very large number of the helmets dug up at Nineveh were made of iron, and some of copper inlaid. Readers of history have only to turn to the pages of Anderson, Fosbroke, Scrivenor, Layard, and others to learn that iron has ever been a most useful and valuable article of commerce.

The Romans proved their constructive ingenuity by the manufacture of those innumerable articles of iron which from time to time have been dug up throughout England, particularly in those districts where woods and forests at one time existed. In Gloucestershire the Forest of Dean for centuries had the extensive furnaces about which so many battles were fought in and out of Parliament, and in Sussex the sites of the ancient ironworks in the Weald can be traced to this day, and will be found described in Lower's "Historical and Archæological Notices," printed in the second volume of the Sussex Collections. In the reign of the Conqueror Gloucestershire possessed a large trade in the forging of iron for the King's navy, and in Edward I.'s time seventy-two furnaces were kept employed. As we progressed, England discovered that the iron we manufactured was wanted for home use, consequently Edward III. prohibited its exportation.

In the accounts for carrying on the war in 1513 there is an item mentioning "nailes and yeran worke," and just thirty years later (according to Holinshed) the first cast-iron cannon was made at Buxted, in Sussex, by Rafe Hoge and Peter Bawde. Among the State Papers there are a quantity relating to the casting of cannon not only in Sussex, but in other counties. The Lamberhurst furnace was a large foundry, for the woods of the Weald were plentiful, and here, at a cost of 11,202*l.*, were produced the 2,500 fine iron railings and seven iron gates, weighing 200 tons and 81 lbs., for the enclosure of Wren's Cathedral of St. Paul's, London. It is worthy of note that as early as 1290 Master Henry of Lewes received a payment for the ironwork of the monument of Henry III. in Westminster Abbey. The parish of Mayfield was famous for its iron; at the palace were preserved many relics, and among these the hammer, anvil, and tongs of St. Dunstan. Lower says "they seem to refer as much to the iron trade, so famous in these parts, as to the alleged proficiency of the Saint in the craft of a blacksmith. The hammer and tongs are of no great antiquity, but the hammer with its iron handle may be considered a mediæval relic." The old legend of St. Dunstan and his successful encounter with "the Evil one" must form part of the history of the blacksmiths, and will not be an uninteresting portion of their "mystery." In 1559 the value of iron and ironwork brought into the port of London, "the excess of which is prejudicial to the realm," is set down in a State Paper to be 19,559*l.* In 1622 Thomas Covell and others received a certificate permitting them to sell round iron shot at 11*l.* per ton.

In the reign of Elizabeth there are two most interesting notices in manuscript. The first of the year 1574, the second of the Armada year 1588. Nowadays we are used to "company promoting," but three centuries ago there was as wild a scheme countenanced by Her Majesty's Ministers as ever was floated to-day. Strype, in his "Annals" (quoting the original MSS.), says "a great project has been carrying on now for two or three years of alchymy, William Medley being the great undertaker to turn iron into copper. Sir Thomas Smith, Secretary of State, had by some experiments made before him a great opinion of it," so had the great Lord Burleigh, the Earl of Leicester, Sir Humphrey Gilbert, and others, each of whom speculated, with the result that Her Majesty (for certain royalties allowed her) granted them a patent in January, 1574, incorporating them as the "Governor and Society of the New Art" . . . "for making copper and quicksilver by the way of transmutation with the commodities growing of that mystery." Twenty persons only were to form the company; to "dig open and work for any mines, owers, and things whatsoever." Sundry sums of 100*l.* each were subscribed by Burleigh, Smith & Co., but "the concern" did not prosper. The assay master at the Tower mint was sent to "the works," and so was Robert Denham, a relative, by the way, of the Sir Wm. Denham who had been seven times Master of the Ironmongers' Company; but somehow or other we fail, as Strype failed with all the papers before him, to learn "the wind up" of what was thought to be "a most splendid investment."

Now in 1588 there was the original certificate given by "John Colman, of the Kane, gent," of "Chardges belonging to a furnace for making a fowndry of iron for one whole weeke" at Canckwood (Cannock Wood?), co. Stafford. According to this document, for one ton the furnace cost 110*s.* 10¼*d.*, and the forge 69*s.* 2*d.*; total, 9*l.* 0*s.* 0¼*d.* Seven years previous to this, the Act of Elizabeth, "Touching yron milles neere unto the Cittie of London and the Ryver of Thames," enacted tha in consequence of the great consumption of wood as fuel for these mills, no woods within 22 miles of the City should be converted "to cole or other fewell for the making of iron or iron mettell in any iron milles furnes or hammer," except the woods of the wealds of Surrey, Sussex, and Kent, and the woods of Christopher Darrell, of Newdigate, Surrey, gent, and who had already preserved his woods for his own iron-works.

Speaking of patents and Acts of Parliament recalls a note or two which may as well be stated here. In 1676 Samuel Hutchinson, citizen and ironmonger of London, had a patent granted to him for his invention, "a newe way of melting downe leade oare into good and mallyable mettall with minerall coales commly called sea coales and pitt coales, which hath byn approved of by many prsons dealing in leade and other artists." In 1766 John Purnell, of Froombridge, Gloucester, ironmaster, invented a new machine for making ship-bolts and rods of iron and steel. Between these dates there were several patents granted to ironmongers, but the patents were for numerous inventions quite apart from the trade.

We have stated that the Ironmongers are known to have existed many years previous to their incorporation in 1463. Now, according to the ancient City records, called "Liber Horn," compiled in the reign of Edward I., (and quoted by Stow and others), the "Feroners," or dealers in iron, about the year 1300 complained to the Mayor (Elias Russel) and the aldermen "for that the smiths of the wealds and other merchants bringing down irons of wheels for carts to the City of London they were much shorter than was anciently, to the great loss and scandal of the whole trade of ironmongers." Whereupon an inquisition was taken, and three rods of the just length of the strytes, and the length and breadth of the gropes belonging to the wheels of carts were presented and sealed with the City seal. One was deposited in the Chamber of London, Guildhall, and the other two handed to John Dode and Robert Paddington, the ironmongers of the market, and John Wymondham, ironmonger of the Bridge, who were accordingly sworn to oversee for the benefit of the trade, and empowered to seize all unjust and less-sized irons in future. This reference is particularly interesting, for it not only proves the existence of "the trade" at least one hundred and sixty years before the incorporation of the Ironmongers, but gives us an insight into the way complaints were redressed nearly six hundred years ago.

In Causton's introduction to "Mildmay on City Elections," we are told that in a few years after the accession of Edward III. a silent revolution had been accomplished—the gildated crafts by the enrolment of the special freemen, householders of the wards each in his mystery, had obtained an exclusively civic importance, paramount to the mixed character of the inhabitants of the wards as civic divisions, and the reconstruction of the City from a territorial to a trading classification had become complete. Thus, in the twenty-fifth year of Edward III., 1351, a precept was directed to the wardens of the City Guilds by the Mayor (which precept formerly had been directed to the men of each ward), and in this precept each of the thirty-three mysteries was directed to select from their number four persons, who were to join the others of the Companies in a consultation with the Mayor and Sheriffs on the business of the City. The Ironmongers accordingly selected their two wardens and two others to represent them, and from this date they claim their existence as a Guild. In 1363 (37 Edward III.), when these Companies were called upon for "an offering" to the

King to enable him to carry on the war in France, the then large sum of 452*l.* 16*s.* was contributed, and the Ironmongers supplied 6*l.* 18*s.* 4*d.* It is worthy of note that upon this occasion in precedency on the list it stood eleventh, while to-day, some 500 years later, its precedency on the list of City Companies is the tenth. Of this precedency, which was a serious question in olden time, we shall have to say a few words later on in our history.

We have now to mention a most interesting circumstance, which has only recently been discovered. Among the enrolled letters at Guildhall which between 1350 and 1370 were sent from the Corporation to many persons, and which Dr. Sharpe, the Records Clerk, so ably edited for the City four years ago, there is one written in French, and dated the 18th of October, the 38th Edward III. (1364), and directed to some persons whose names have not been preserved, but then residents at Bury—probably Bury St. Edmonds, in Suffolk—"desiring them to assist Thomas de Mildenhale, citizen and ironmonger of London, to recover his runaway apprentice, Andrew, the son of William Bruwere, who is understood to be staying in the town of Bury, in such manner as they would wish their folk to be treated in like case or weightier. The Lord have them ever in his keeping." We are not told, and are not likely to know now, whether this runaway "merry" Andrew was brought back, and, if so, how the Chamberlain received him. In subsequent days a runaway apprentice would have "little ease" at the hands of the Guildhall caretaker of a citizen's conscience.

We shall include in this second chapter of our history another most interesting document which Mr. Riley found when making his extracts from the Guildhall treasures a few years ago. It is nothing more or less than the appraisement of the goods and chattels of Stephen le Northerne, in the thirtieth year of Edward III. (1356), and gives us a very curious picture of what an ironmonger's shop contained at that date. It would appear that the goods were in the house of one John Leche, in the parish of St. Michael, Cornhill, on June 6 that year, and that the appraisers were William Sunnyng, carpenter, Robert de Blithe, "brasyere," Robert Russe, "brasyere," Henry Clement and Stephen Basham, "lockyers" (locksmiths), and Adam Wayte, "upholder." The total value of the household goods and stock-in-trade came to the sum of 9*l.* 14*s.* 2*d.*, but even this amount was a large one in those days. Among the articles enumerated and appraised we find five carpets, 7*s.*; five bankeres, (bench-covers), 12 quyshynes (cushions), and one dosere (tapestry hanging), 3*s.* 9*d.*; three tablecloths and one towel, 21*d.*; one surcoat, 8*s.*; one aumbrey (portable cupboard) and chest, 18*d.*; one balance, called an "auncere" (weighing-machine), 12*d.*; pair of iron gauntlets and pair of bracers (for the arms), 6*d.*; 20 lbs. pewter, 2*s.* 11*d.*; two querne (or mill) stones, 18*d.*; three brass pots, two pitchers, a basin, seven brass plates, nine pieces of holdshrof, 19*s.* 11*d.*; feather bed, three carpets, three sheets, 9*s.* 6*d.*; two balances, 6*s.*; trivet and four iron slegges (sledge-hammers), 3*s.* 6*d.*; two plonchones (iron punches) and four cart-strokes (tires), 3*s.* 8*d.*; pair of irons for Eucharist, five fire-forks, four beynges, one tin pan, six latches for doors, four small goldsmiths' anvils, two kerfsheres (chaff-shears), 5*s.*; eight pairs of kemstercombs (wool-combers), and one boweshawe (bowshave), 11*d.*; old iron and balance, 6*s.* 8*d.*; two iron spits and iron for bedsteads, 5*s.* 8*d.*; fifteen battle-axes, 7*s.*;

four hatches and nine pair of hinges, 6*s.*; two small andirons, twelve hatchets, five pickaxes, seven carpenters' axes, three twybilles, three woodbilles, four masons' axes (old), pair of pincers, flesh-hook, &c., 10*s.* 4*d.*; twelve dozen hinges, 5*s.*; ten pairs linch-pins, nine pairs of bar-hooks, 6*s.*; iron grate, anvil, &c., 2*s.* 3*d.*; thirty-three pairs of okees (ornamental mouldings), 6*s.*; twenty bolts and sockets, 6*s.*; twelve pairs of Utt garnets, eleven pairs of Ambry garnets, ten plate-locks, 8*s.* 6*d.*; five latches, iron chisel, 120 keys, twelve cart-clouts (axle-tree plates), 3*s.*; pikestaff, 4*d.*; sixty columns (axle trees) for wheels, three barrels and two vats, 2*s.* 3*d.*; pair of mustard querns (mills), 6*d.*: mincing-bowl and shoe-horn, 1*d.*; bacinet, dagger, and buckler, 5*s.*; wooden bed-stead, 2*s.*; &c.

This inventory is very curious, and, as inventories of so early a date are very rare, we could not resist the temptation of quoting one, especially when it related to an ironmonger's shop. Now, it appears that the whole of these goods and chattels, together with one tenement, three shops, and one alley, situated in the parish of St. Michael, Cornhill, and valued at fourteen shillings yearly (rents in Cornhill were reasonable in those days), were delivered over to Simon Palmer, "pelterer," and William Sunnyng, "carpenter," by the Mayor and Aldermen, to be holden in trust for the use of Alice, the daughter of John Leche aforesaid, when she came of age. As the premises appear to have been shortly afterwards burnt to the ground, the trustees had to rebuild, and on folio 45 of the Corporation Letter Book G Mr. Riley found the cost of such restoration.

In our first chapter we stated it was in 1377 that by enactment the Common Council and other officials of the City were directed to be elected from the mysteries instead of by the Wards, as theretofore. This privilege, although only temporarily enjoyed as regarded the Council, yet has continued, so far as the Liverymen being the elective body of the City officials, down to the present time, notwithstanding that 500 years have passed by since the passing of the Act; and, looking at the list of names of the persons chosen and the many notable individuals, styled by old Stow under the heading, "Honor of citizens and worthinesse of men in the same," there are few persons who carefully and without prejudice study the facts but will agree with us that the Livery have never neglected their duty, but have, as a rule, only elected those persons who would do their duty to their country, to their Sovereign, and to their brethren in the City. We sincerely trust that, whenever any elective franchise is conferred upon the Londoners at large, they will execute their trust with as good and unbiased a judgment. In our next chapter we shall tell how the Ironmongers carried out their trust after their foundation as a Guild and an Incorporated Company of the City of London.

CHAPTER III.

THE WORSHIPFUL COMPANY OF IRONMONGERS.

ALTHOUGH existing records do not give us all the information we should like to have about the ancient history of the Guilds, we have, nevertheless, been able to show that by their joining in the election of the City officials in the year 1351, and choosing four of their members (John Deynes and Richard de Eure, wardens, and Henry de Ware and William Fromond), "the wisest and most sufficient" in the Guild, to treat with the Mayor and Sheriffs upon the "serious business" of the City, that the Ironmongers were duly recognised thus early as a firmly-established brotherhood.

The "market," or special place of business of the fraternity, was, as we have said, in the neighbourhood of the City Guildhall, and hence the existing name of Ironmonger Lane, which is a thoroughfare out of Cheapside, on the north side, and the next turning to the Old Jewry westward, between which streets to this day stands a church, known as St. Olave's (about to be removed), the predecessors of which —St. Martin's, Ironmonger's Lane, and St. Olave—contained the remains of several eminent ironmongers, including William Dikeman, "Feroner," one of the sheriffs, 1367; Robert Havelocke, 1390; Thomas Michell, 1527; Richard Chamberlain, 1562. At what date the craft left this neighbourhood is unknown. We know they possessed the Ironmongers' Hall, more east, near Billiter Street, in the middle of the fifteenth century, about which district the members individually may have carried on business; Strype, however, stating that when they removed from their old market they took up a position in Thames Street, wherein to this day, as is well known, the iron wharves and warehouses are numerous and extensive.

The precedency question in the olden time was a momentous one for the City Guilds, and led to many conflicts between the members of certain companies, which will be mentioned when speaking of "the Livery" and "apprentices" hereafter. It is worthy of note here to remark that in the year 1376 (7), the fiftieth of Edward III., forty-eight Guilds elected 148 of their members as the Common Council, when the Ironmongers, standing the thirty-fifth in the list, elected four of their number. We imagine that no actual precedency was here followed, for in subsequent lists the "great" companies contained first thirteen names, and eventually twelve, in which the Ironmongers stood eighth, eleventh, and, finally, tenth, a position assigned them not so much for their wealth, but probably for their respectability, or, as old Stow says, "the worthiness of the men," and the power they possessed.

Again, from these great companies the Lord Mayor was

ANCIENT SILVER-GILT SALT-CELLAR. (See page 21.)

A FIFTEENTH-CENTURY MAPLE-WOOD MAZER-BOWL. (See page 47.)

always chosen. The first Mayor was Henry Fitzalwyn, "Draper," near the London Stone, which is an ancient City relic still existing (but not on its original site) in Cannon Street, not many yards from the office of THE IRONMONGER, in which this history is first published exactly 700 years afterwards, for Fitzalwyn was first chosen in 1189, and continued to hold office twenty-four successive years. As we have said, the Lord Mayor was always "one of the Twelve"; but in 1742 Sir Robert Wilmot, "Cooper," declining to be "translated" to the Clothworkers (as was the custom when the Mayor elect was of a minor company), and there being no law to compel him, he was consequently the first Mayor not of the great companies; and it is a curious fact that Wilmot's predecessor in office was an ironmonger, and to this day the Coopers and the Ironmongers are associated in the Irish estate.

After a lapse of 500 years it will be interesting to many, and to those who object to oath-taking in particular, if we give in its original form the wording of the Ironmongers' Warden's oath required to be taken before admission in the fiftieth year of Edward III. Its quaint phraseology must be our excuse for the transcript:—"Ye shall swere that ye shall wele and treuly ov'see the Craft of Iremongers' wher of ye be chosen Wardeyn for the yeere. And all the goode reules and ordynces of the same craft that been approved here be the Court, and noon other, ye shal kepe and doo to be kept. And all the defautes that ye fynde in the same Craft ydon to the Chambleyn of ye Citee for the tyme beyng, ye shal wele and treuly P'sente. Sparyng noo man for favor ne grevyng noo p'sone for hate. Extorcion ne wrong under colour of your office ye shall non doo, nethir to noo thing thot shalbe ayenst the State, peas, and profite of oure Sovereyn Lord the Kyng or to the Citee ye shall not consente, but for the tyme that ye shalbe in office in all things thot shalbe longyng unto the same craft after the lawes and ffranchises of the seide Citee welle and laufully ye shal have you. So helpe you God and all Seyntes."

In 1397, one of the years of "Dick Whittington" as Lord Mayor, a curious case came before the Court of Aldermen for decision. William Sevenoake, a native of Sevenoaks, in Kent, and who, subsequent to the date we mention, was Sheriff and Mayor of London, and founder of the schools and almshouses at Sevenoaks, prayed the Court to be enrolled on the Grocers' Company, notwithstanding in his apprenticeship his master Hugh de Boys was called an ironmonger. The Grocers having proved the facts, William was accordingly entered as a grocer, and 40*s.* paid for the privilege.

Before their incorporation, the Ironmongers were represented by three Mayors of London, viz., Sir Richard Marlow, 1409-10, and again, 1417-18, and by Sir John Hatherley, 1442-43, and yet, after their incorporation, and not until the year 1566-67 did another ironmonger fill the "chair," although several sheriffs represented the Guild both before and after their charter was granted.

Herbert, the Guildhall librarian of half a century ago, speaking of the compulsory enrolment of the Companies' charters, "regretted exceedingly that so little could be found about the ancient state of the City Guilds among the State papers and records preserved by the nation." If the zealous literary citizen had only known then what we know to-day he would not only have regretted, but denounced in the strongest terms (as we do now), the gross mismanagement of the State Paper Office in the past and the red-tapeism of the present time, the former losing to us for ever most valuable records, the latter placing every obstacle possible in the way of the documents now remaining being conveniently used by historians, the publication of the contents thereof greatly helping towards their future preservation. In our searches at the Public Record Office for the purpose of this history, we have experienced this inconvenience, and we certainly consider it should not exist in a Government institution supported by the public. When we find the authorities at the British Museum, and the Guildhall, and other repositories open to us, and giving every facility with their records, which, after all, embrace priceless treasures and quite as worthy of safe custody, the restrictions placed upon literary research by the Master of the Rolls and the Record Office officials is really worthy a Royal Commission of inquiry.

When Henry VII. entered the City in 1485 the Guilds supplied 435 members to meet the King, and of these ten were Ironmongers. In the year 1504 there was a subscription of the sixty-one Companies, amounting to 313*l.* 16*s.* 8*d.*, towards the erection of the kitchen and offices at Guildhall, and 5*l.* was the sum the Ironmongers gave. It must be borne in mind that in those days a small sum went a long way.

We now arrive at an interesting period of the Company's history. Eight years previous to obtaining their charter of incorporation the Ironmongers obtained a grant of arms. Both charter and grant have been repeatedly exhibited and described, and beautiful facsimiles of the two documents will be found in Mr. G. R. French's "Catalogue of the Ironmongers' Exhibition of Antiquities," in 1861, a most sumptuously printed and privately circulated work, and now very scarce.

By warrant dated September 1, the thirty-fourth of Henry VI. (1455), "Lancastre, Kyng of Armes," and the College of Arms granted "Unto the honurable Crafte and felasship of the ffraunchised men of Iremongers of the Citie of London a token of armes, that is to sey: Silver a cheveron of Gowles sitte betwene three gaddes of steie of asure, on the cheueron three swevells of golde; with two lizardes of theire owne kynde encoupled with gowlys, on the helmet."

The two lizards on the helmet, it must be borne in mind, represent the crest. "The Crafte" and their successors were to hold and enjoy these arms "for evermore," and the privilege of using a tabard upon all state occasions. Clarenceux, King at Arms, inspected the original grant in 1530-31, and signed its confirmation, and in 1560 William Hervy, another Clarenceux, curiously enough upon inspecting the same document, found the patent "to be without good authoryte," and therefore, either to ease his conscience or that of the College, or for the more likely reason to be mentioned presently, confirms once again the same grant of "armes, helme, and crest" to "the Corporacon, Company, and Comynalty, and to their successors for evermore," to use the same "in shylde banners, standardes, and otherwyse," and "without impedyment or interuption of any person or persons," for the confirmation of which privilege, already enjoyed for one hundred years, the Ironmongers' books, Mr. Nicholl tells us, show that "Mayster Clarensys" received thirty-seven shillings, and "his svant for bringing them hom" twelve pence for his own use.

Notwithstanding the official granting and confirmation, another gentleman from the college, this time the Richmond Herald, inspected the same document, and he too did the Company the honour in 1634 of again "confirming" the same grants, so that it is impossible to deny to the Ironmongers the right and privilege of bearing arms; and one fact is certain, if ever a Corporation or Brotherhood possessed appropriate armorials suggestive of their trade it is this Guild, which cannot be said of the armorial shields of many other City Companies.

Now, we have gone into this matter of the granting of the arms and the three confirmations beyond the usually allotted space in histories for the simple reason that one of the most extraordinary circumstances in connection with heraldic grants has yet to be explained. The Ironmongers' Company, although possessing a grant which has been thrice confirmed by the College, and in which the two lizards appear as a crest, never received from either of the Heralds who were good enough for a consideration to inspect and confirm an authority which each ought to have given, to use "supporters" to the armorial shield, or, if the Company had no right to use them, to inquire the reason why, &c., when such were assumed.

The Company adopting the supporters, two lizards, as in the crest, Edmondson, another Herald, in 1780 actually stated in his Heraldic work that they were given the Company in one of the confirmations! In 1812 the question again came before Garter, King of Arms, when the Collegians were good enough to say that the Ironmongers might have a "confirmation" of the supporters upon paying the modest fee of 73*l*. It is needless to say that the Company declined to pay this (in our opinion) extortionate demand, and so to this day (as it has exercised from a period long before this century dawned) the Ironmongers bear their supporters, as only true citizens should.

It may be interesting to note here that in many armorial shields of private families there are similarities to that of the Ironmongers', except that, in place of the chevron between three gads of steel, there are a chevron between three billets of wood, and it is particularly interesting to call attention to the fact that such a coat is to be found in a seal dated 1359, and still more curious that in the deed on which this seal appears three ironmongers are mentioned: John Deynes, William Dikeman, and Henry de Ware. This was nearly a century previous to the Company receiving a grant of arms.

The lizards, now used by the Ironmongers as crest and supporters, were also used when naming their manor in Ireland in the reign of James I., now known as the "Manor of Lizard," and about which we shall speak hereafter. Mr. Herbert, fifty years ago, remarks:—"What are in the arms termed 'lizards,' we may rather imagine were intended to represent salamanders—a creature supposed, like iron, to live unhurt in fire." Pennant says:—"The frolicsome agility of lizards enlivens the dried banks in hot climates, and the great affection which some of them show to mankind should further engage our regard and attention." Another writer quaintly suggests that the dear little animal not only loves iron, but likes it hot, eating it with a relish, and digests it with ease. See also the head-piece to Herbert's "History."

Under the armorials is the Company's motto, and that is, appropriately, "God is our strength." It is not known when this was assumed, but the date is modern, for anciently—at all events, in the seventeenth century—the Ironmongers' motto was "Assher Dure," which a well-known antiquary translates as "steel endures," and will be found in the heraldic volume of Companies' arms in the British Museum.

A most important step was now taken, which in the history of the Guild at once entitled it to the style of "worshipful." In 1463 it obtained a charter of incorporation. Written in Latin, it is not a lengthy document, but is interesting, and prettily illuminated in gold and colours, with the royal arms within the initial letter "E" of Edwardus, and another shield of the Company's arms in the margin beneath. Pendant is a fine specimen of the royal seal of England, circular in sire, in green wax, dated Westminster, March 20, the third year of Edward IV., then 1462, but, since the alteration of the calendar, now 1463. The King grants: "To our well-beloved and faithful liegemen all the freemen of the mystery and art of Iremongers of our City of London and suburbs thereof" the rights and privileges to be a body corporate for evermore, to have a master and two wardens (who are named as Richard Flemming, alderman; and Nicholas Marchall and Robert Toke) and a commonalty, with perpetual succession, under the name of "the master and keepers or wardens and commonalty of the mystery or art of Ironmongers of London," to have a common seal, make ordinances, to purchase and hold lands and tenements to the value of 10 marks yearly.

The day upon which the Guild received their incorporation charter they, doubtless, celebrated with all the ceremonials and festivities which we, 400 years afterwards, indulge in to-day, and they recorded in their books a resolution: "That they shalle holde and kepe the said feste for their principall fesst, evermore."

Ironmongers' Hall in Fenchurch Street will be described in another chapter, but we may as well state that the site of the present building was granted in the year 1457 by the executors of Alice Stivard, the widow of Sir John Stivard, Knight, to the nineteen "citizen and ironmongers" mentioned (among whom were the three named in the charter), and that in the Company's books occurs the entry, "Bought by the for wreten ffelowshipp and paid fore, and also posesson taken the XX daie of Octobr the XXXVI yer of King Henry the VI."

Now, what do our reforming friends in 1889 say to this? There is nothing said about trusts here. It is as much the Company's freehold and belongs to them, the "root and branch" descendants, as ever the commonest article that may be purchased (and paid for, mark ye!) by any citizen and working-man to-day. So, in simply quoting the purchase here, we do so to put all reformers on their guard not to be so ready to make hay (by their seizure) before the sun shines on assumed or presumed rights.

But we will go a little further. The Company did not buy without legal aid, for the books show "lernyd counsaile at the purchas makyng" received not only 26*s.* 8*d.* for their advice and labours, but there was paid "at taverns dyvers tymes" for refreshments to the same gentlemen the large sum of 3*s.* 6*d.*

Having purchased a house and garden, and regularly gone

into housekeeping, the Ironmongers began their furnishing in humble style. Among the first articles purchased were the following:—

x stoles	iijs.	iiijd.
i fire forke		
i pr tongs	xjs.	vijd.
i pr andyrons		
i rake		
vij candlestickes	iijs.	iiijd.
i table and ij tressels	iiijs.	vjd.
i caudron in a furneys in the kechen ..		vijd.
i pr bed bords in the chamber		xxd.
i water tankard		xvijd.
i cheste in the boterye, bounded wth yron ..	ijs.	

And the same accounts tell us that "the alderman and the bedill at ye possessyon takyng" received 2s. 6d. "For brede and ale at our possession takyn" 22d. was spent, while "barge hyre at twoo tymes' cost 14s., but there is no evidence what for, or where to the barges were so employed.

It must not be said that the Worshipful Company of Ironmongers commenced incorporated existence extravagantly. And we shall be able to show in our next chapter that, as they began so they continued, careful in the management of their charity trusts, and frugal in all matters pertaining to their government.

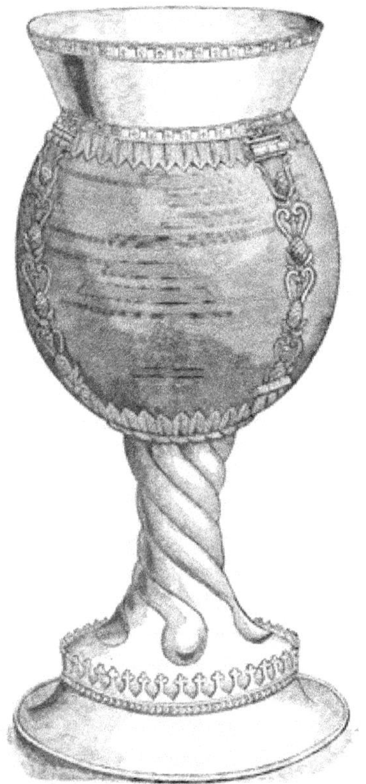

A Sixteenth-century Cocoa-nut Cup or Hanap.

CHAPTER IV.

FOUR HUNDRED YEARS OF THE IRONMONGERS' HISTORY.—I.

ALTHOUGH Mr. Alderman Cotton, one of the Parliamentary City Companies' Commissioners, reported five years ago "that the returns made to the Commission show conclusively that the members of the Livery Companies were never exclusively of the trade the name of which was borne by their Company, and that for about 400 years the larger proportion of the members have not pretended to follow the crafts of their Companies," and that "the Livery Companies are not to be classed with friendly or benevolent societies, with monastic institutions, or with political or other clubs, but rather approached the character of a masonic body," exercising in the past and at the present time a very good and important moral influence not only upon citizens and City life, but upon public life generally," and foremost in the promotion of education and charitable acts, we shall show that, like many other of the Companies, the Ironmongers' has never proved indifferent to its particular trade or its kindred associations.

It was contended before the Commissioners in 1882 that the whole of the charters of the Companies are bad because the King parted with his right to grant charters conferring the right of search. Without attempting to enter into the question, or debate the correctness of such an assertion, as only a lawyer could and would in "the good old times," upon the power of the sovereign to make a grant which has stood the test of centuries, no such right is to be found in either of the Ironmongers' charters. The records of the Company show that statutory legislation for the protection and regulation of the iron trade was enacted in the reign of Henry IV., Richard III., Henry VIII., and Edward VI., and that on certain occasions this Company have laid abuses of the trade before the Common Council that they might deal therewith, this company not having the power in itself. Amongst its own commonalty only the Ironmongers' exercised supervision and control of trading, but as none of the trade joined the Company other than of their own free will and for their own good, obedience to such control can only be regarded as voluntary, and not as infringing the liberty of the subject contrary to the provisions of Magna Charta.

We therefore desire in the present chapter, while giving a chronicle of the Ironmongers' progress during the past 400 years, to show that the old City Guild has a history in many respects peculiarly its own, and that since its incorporation it has frequently proved most valuable to the State, the City, and the people.

And yet the Ironmongers as brethren have had their troubles. Witness the City Sheriff of 1479, Robert Byfield by name and Ironmonger by Company, who, with Sir Bartholomew James, the then Lord Mayor, attended prayers at St. Paul's Cathedral, and had the audacity to kneel too close to his Civic Majesty. His Lordship chid him for the affront; Mr. Sheriff resented the scolding, and the end of the extraordinary squabble was that the Court of Aldermen tried the case, and fined Mr. Byfield, who, says Stow, "payd 50*l*. towards the water conduits," one of which, the great conduit in Cheapside, was then building. Our Sheriff, who resided in Tower Street, did not long survive the trial, for he died in 1482, and by his will proved he was far from being unmindful of religious or charitable influences, for he not only founded a chapel and made many bequests, but did not forget his poorer brethren in Fenchurch Street.

But not alone and personally have the Ironmongers suffered. Our early Monarchs appear to have considered the rich and powerful Citizens a fair field for plunder. While Royalty was privileged to run to excesses, and by extravagance spent the income their loyal subjects provided, the Citizens, because they exercised their moral and more business-like spirit of showing a balance on the right side of the ledger, were made victims of repeated extortions. It is no use denying, and unjust to deny, that our Sovereigns have so loved London as to sacrifice their comfort or their greed by visiting it for other than personal motives, and the records show but too plainly that Royalty in the past has depended upon the wealth of "a nation of shopkeepers" for a constant supply of the "needful." The Royal draw upon the City purse commenced early in London's existence, and great has been the loss to the Citizens; and yet to-day there are those who still clamour for the extinction of the very source which has kept the nation alive! Our remarks are not overdrawn, as our proofs are many—too many, in fact, to be detailed at large. One or two must suffice now.

Beginning, then, more than 350 years ago, King Henry VIII. set a bad example to his descendants. Having asked the City for 20,000*l*.—only as a loan, of course—in the year 1523, he, the more readily to raise it, "comandyed to have all the money and platt that was belonging to every hawlle or craft," and so the poor Ironmongers had to pay up among the other Companies. The book sorrowfully records, "At the whyche comandmentt he had all oure money," and that amounting to only 25*l*. 1*s*. 2*d*., the plate was pawned or sold, realising 46*l*. more, or a total of 71*l*. 14*s*. 2*d*.; and even then, not being satisfied, twenty of the richest members of the Company "lent" him out of their own pockets something like 190*l*., "Mr. Willm Denham oure Warden" heading the list with 30*l*. We hope he was repaid, but we doubt it.

The King having obtained this "little loan" so easily did not forget to be "a suitor" to the City again; but the next time the Ironmongers went to the Pawnbrokers was in 1544, when they "layd to plege, the xxij. day of May," their ewers, salts, and cups, to provide "xiiij. men in harnes to goe over the see wth the Kyngs army in to France, that was iiij. bowmen and x. byll men" fully equipped for service. Now we do not intend to quote every occasion when the Sovereign borrowed money, but a few selected cases will tell the tale. In 1575 a precept from the Lord Mayor commanded the Company to assist the Queen's demand by paying 60*l*., coolly adding, "if youe have not soe moche in store then you shale borrowe the same at ynterest at thonly costs and lossis of yor hall." Next year the Queen commanded the City to raise and hold in readiness for her 140,000*l.*, and a few years later, in 1588, the celebrated Armada'year, when every county in England lent its thousands to assist in the defence of the nation, and the Companies of the City advanced 51,900*l.*, we find the Ironmongers' proportion was 2,300*l.* ("The City Guilds Subscription Lists," in "The Western Antiquary," May, 1888), raised among fourteen of the wealthiest members. In 1598 the Queen's Privy Council sent for 20,000*l.* more, and the Ironmongers lent 880*l.* In 1614, the treasury being empty, and Parliament dissolved, the King asked for 100,000*l.*; but the City was far from prosperous that year· Government demands, the Ulster and Virginia plantations, and other calls had drained the City purse; and it was only after several meetings that the Ironmongers obliged His Majesty by making "a benevolence" of 179*l.* And when, in 1620, another demand was made, and the Company granted 170*l.*, the members were compelled for a time to be so economical that not only were all their dinners stopped, but they actually fined each other so that the current expenses could be paid. And still the obnoxious and oppressive precepts poured in. In 1627, in 1628, in 1630, the citizens were truly "dearly beloved" to the King, and when, in 1640 and 1642, the Parliamentary demands for another trifling "loan" of 100,000*l.* made matters more and more disheartening, the Ironmongers were forced to part with 3,400*l.*, and another advance a little later made the Government a debtor to the Company in the year 1652 of no less a sum than 9,536*l.* 3*s.* 7*d.* If we calculate what was owing to the other Corporations at the same time at only half this sum each, is it to be wondered at that there were civil wars, or that the extravagances of the "Merry Monarch" and his saintly brother James brought about in succession the shutting up of the Exchequer and the revolution of two centuries ago?

The Ironmongers had all along proved to be such true friends to the State that they found out to their cost, and too late, that they had not been true to themselves. Their account with the Government and their Royal masters of fifty years before still remained unsettled, and to so low a pitch had their exchequer fallen that in 1691 they were again compelled to pawn their plate for 253*l.*, and no longer trust to the promises or bonds of their debtors. And so, striking off the balance of 5,000*l.* as a bad debt, they determined in future to trust only those who were trustworthy. But even the loss or money, and having to pawn their plate and valuables, were not their only troubles. The harassing demands of the State at times were so oppressive that it makes us wonder the City did not revolt sooner than it did and shut its gates to tyranny as Derry did in 1688. Only one example of oppression need I give here. In 1675 the Hearth Tax collector called in Fenchurch Street and demanded 4*l.* 16*s.* for "chimney money" for two empty houses, belonging to the Company, then standing between the present Queen Victoria and Thames Streets. The Ironmongers declined to pay the demand, whereupon (says the record) "he (the collector) did, wth his consorts and constable, goe upp into the hall and took away one of the Company's salts." This was distressing with a vengeance, everyone will admit, and, notwithstanding that we think empty houses to-day should pay their share of taxation and thus lighten parochial rates, we do not advocate the sharp practice of King Charles's collector.

Let us now take a rapid review of the Company's history as applicable to the trade. If they did not possess the right of search or the power over the trade generally, like some of the other Guilds, they by advice and action with the Corporation and Companies have upon many occasions proved most beneficial and valuable. The earliest ordinances of the Guild are of the date 1498. They provide for the elections of the Master and Wardens "wth tokens of garlands on their heds," the charge of purchasing "clothing or lyvery" for the brotherhood at the drapers' shops at Blackwell Hall (on or near the site of the present Guildhall Library); the settling of the dinners, when the member paid 2*s*., "and for the wyf if she be att the dyner xii*d*." (which is not an ironmonger's wife's privilege at the present time); those freemen warned to attend the Hall and disobeying to be fined 4*d*., and the wardens 2*s*.; none to offer insult to their brethren; "no member to sue a brother for debt without leave of the wardens"; apprentices to be admitted to the fellowship "having served his tyme well and truly"; "straungers or foreigners (that is to say, those not already of the City) may be elected if introduced by four creditable liverymen; "the Wardens, once in every two years at least, to search all manner of weights and measures that be used in the same felashippe, and when they find any default to levy fines at the discression of the master and wardens"; apprentices to be enrolled at Guildhall within the first year, and to be registered in the Company's book; "no person in the felashippe shall take noon apprentice excepte he have sewertie and bond for him in C[li] sterling"; and no apprentice to be "under 14 years of age, and for no lesse terme than X yeres, except it be his first apprentice taken for necessitee, and for him he shel ax licence of the wardeyns," and every apprentice his master shall advise to be "resonable and honest," and shall see that he have clean and sound "hosyn, doblett, shirtis, and other necessaries," . . . "to kepe hym from colde and wete," and by no means to suffer "his here to growe to long." Finally, every member of the fellowship, whether in or out of the clothing (that is to say, liveryman or freeman), was required "to appear iiij. tymes in the yeere at the foure principal Courts, and these iiij. Courts ben ordeyned alway to endure to Goddes pleasir principally, and to redresse the maters that be not wele used, and to kepe pece and gode rewle among us," and at these Courts all arrearages were to be paid—the master, 12*d*.; the present or past wardens, 8*d*.; the clothing (or liveryman), 6*d*.; and the yeomanry (or freeman), 4*d*.; and the wardens not to see the yeomanry decay.

Such then is an abstract of the earliest ordinances of the Ironmongers. At the present time the Company consists of a master, two wardens, the livery (all of whom comprise the Court, and, therefore, unlike any other City Company, who have a livery and a court of assistants as well), and the yeomanry, or freemen generally, over which presides a warden chosen by and from themselves at Easter, yearly. Of these we shall speak in another chapter.

The ordinances were revised and approved by the Lord Chancellor and Justices in February 1581, when the rules were either modified or extended. The elections are set forth; the four quarterly courts were settled, and at which the master paid his quarterage money of 16*d*.; the warden, 12*d*.; the liveryman, 9*d*. and the freemen, 4*d*. The apprentice always to be of the age not exceeding twenty-four when his term expired. The stranger or foreigner when admitted to pay 20*l.* The search of weights and measures to be once a year, or oftener, in the shops of the fellowship, and false ones destroyed, and fines of 40*s.* to the Company to be inflicted. Other special ordinances will be alluded to in another chapter.

The Company in 1549 interested themselves in the passing of the Act against the forging of iron gads instead of gads of steel, and six years later there are several entries relating to the coal meterage, which the Company had to superintend until the reign of James I. In 1557, when the rules of the newly-founded Bridewell at Blackfriars were made, and to which prison rogues and apprentices formerly, and of late years unmanageable City apprentices only, have been sent by the Chamberlain, it was specially provided in the governing of "the nail-house" that "to you is given authority to make sale of all such nayls as shall be made in this house, so the same be done according to the order taken with the Company of Ironmongers, which is, that (they giving to this house as the people of the same may by their travail reasonably live) shall before all men have all the nails that are made therein, and have one month's day of payment for the same." An inventory of all iron and nails, smithies, hammers, anvils, bellows, and tools to be truly kept, &c., and proper workmen appointed to oversee the idle apprentices' work. In 1579 there were at Bridewell what in 1597 were called "art masters," or those who had charge of trade apprentices, and among these were the naylors and pinmakers. In 1598 "Spanish needles" were made in the prison; in 1602 the pinners' boys numbered fourteen, and in 1604 there were to be forty.

In the first year of Queen Elizabeth, 1558, the new Timber Act received special consideration from the Company, for it concerned the ironworks. In 1561 they took action against one of the freemen, Clement Cornwall, about whom a complaint was lodged for selling inferior goods at Lewes Fair, and three years later, at the instance of the yeomanry, the Court ordered that at fairs or elsewhere their members must sell nails six score to the hundred, and not five score as formerly. In 1569 the Founders' Company fell out with the wardens of the Ironmongers', which was settled by the aldermen, and ten years later three members of each Company of Ironmongers and Grocers were ordered to attend between the hours of 7 A.M. and 6 P.M. at the Bishop Gate of the City, to inspect and search every person and see that their "apparil, swords, daggers, or bucklers, w[t] long pikes, great ruffs or long cloakes, or carry thear swordes close under their armes or the poyntes upward" were as by the late proclamation provided. In 1612 the Ironmongers, Blacksmiths, and Carpenters had many meetings, and passed special resolutions jointly on the then serious question of the importation of rod iron and a newly granted patent, and it is interesting to note that the then senior warden of the Company was the young gentleman who misbehaved himself at Lewes Fair in 1561, as already mentioned. In 1623 the Cutlers joined the Ironmongers, and obtained from the Corporation the by-law that all strangers or others should be compelled, as heretofore, to bring cutlery and iron wares to Leadenhall to be examined. This new by-law caused the Corporation and Companies much trouble to carry out, but it continued a City ordinance down to the year 1665.

In 1636 another trouble arose. A petition to the King by

the shipwrights complained of the making of nails "of the worst iron, of lesse weight, strength and goodnes then in former tyme." As the petitioners stated the deceits were committed by "wholesale men who employed poor smiths," there was evidently a case of "sweating" in those days. For this the Company were called upon to appear before the Privy Council, where, of course, they would plead that they had no power over the trade generally. Four years afterwards the old complaint of the strangers, Leadenhall, underselling, &c., the Ironmongers were brought before the Corporation, and it was ordered that the Company should, when necessary, take possession, &c. The same year, too, the Company had to take notice of a monopoly granted by the King to his gunfounder, of cast-iron goods, which the Company were fortunate enough to get "called in and overthrown." In 1657 John Richardson, a pinmaker by trade and Ironmonger by Company, prayed to be translated to the newly-formed Company of Pinmakers; but as by his copy of freedom he was to hold chiefly of the fellowship of Ironmongers, the Court of the Company refused assent. This custom is a peculiar one to the Ironmongers, and has often proved a bar to progress to those desiring to join other Guilds where promotion is more rapid.

CHAPTER V.

FOUR HUNDRED YEARS OF THE IRONMONGERS' HISTORY.—II.

IT has been asserted by some of the most violent opposers to the Corporation of London and the City Guilds that the Companies are part and parcel of the Corporation, that they were incorporated for the special benefit of the trades the names of which they are known by, that they once were, and should still be, solely composed of such trades' members, and their property devoted to the artisans of such trades. Now, with all due respect to such arguments and those who may argue on these grounds, we must at once point out what is always considered to be the most sensible view of the question—that circumstances alter cases, and the merits of each case deserve to be considered separately. Were it otherwise there would be at once an end of our freedom and birthright, Magna Charta, and everything else.

In our previous chapters we have shown that the Ironmongers' charter makes no mention of the Guild as specially incorporated for trade purposes or for the trade's sole benefit, and that the earliest by-laws simply conferred the right of search and inspecting all weights and measures "used in the same feloshippe," and consequently did not apply to the trade in general. In fact there was, and still remains, no compulsion upon an ironmonger to join the Company, although in ancient times, by charter-rights, he would be compelled to become a freeman of the City, which, as we have already stated, did not constitute him free of a Company as well. The Ironmongers' charter was confirmed by Philip and Mary, June 20, 1558; by Queen Elizabeth, November 12, 1560; by James I., June 25, 1604; and by James II., November 19, 1687. The grant of this last-mentioned letters patent was made to the Companies generally after the stormy events of the previous four years, and as some reparation for the gross injustice done to his subjects by Charles II., when, under the power of the writ of *quo warranto*, he seized the City charters and disfranchised the very men who had been his best friends. This act of the "Merry Monarch," and the shutting up of the Exchequer, the ruin of the goldsmiths and bankers, and the continuous oppression of the citizens by his brother James brought about sooner than royalty expected the destruction of the King, "the glorious Revolution of 1688," and the accession of William III. on December 12 of that year, from which time, and by special Act in his second year, the Companies have been restored to their ancient position and privileges. And we firmly believe the lessons then learnt by the partisans of Charles and James, and handed down to their descendants, have not been forgotten by those still living in the Jubilee year of Queen Victoria. In addition to these special charters there was yet another

A Carved Wood Ostrich, as used in the Lord Mayor's Pageant of 1629. (See pages 33–35.)

A Bronze Token, representing the Geffery Almshouses, erected 1713–14. (See page 55.)

grant made, which, as regards their estates, is a complete answer to those who to-day say the Ironmongers' property is not their own. It is "a perpetuitie" made to them and their successors for ever by James I., dated August 4, 1619.

Exactly 300 years ago the ancient City of Chester was represented in its Mayoralty chair by an ironmonger, whose son upset the good people of the City by retailing ironmongers' wares, to the prejudice of the Citizens, who, by a grant from Queen Elizabeth in 1561, had been exempted from a duty of 2s. per ton upon iron imported there. And in the same year of 1589 one Peter Newall, or Newgall, an assistant to his father-in-law, Mr. Bavand, who appears to have enjoyed the distinction of being "an ironmonger, a vintner, a mercer, and a retayler of manye comodities," complained that David Lloyd, "a retaylinge draper," had "usurped the name of merchant," for which wrongdoing the Privy Council, the Secretary of State, the Master of the Rolls, and all the machinery of the law was set in motion that "the drifte of the said Lloyd shalbe ripte upp and viewed into," and the injury to the Citizens repaired. In Buckingham, both in 1691 and 1706, two members of the Blunt family were admitted into the Mercers' Company "to follow the trade of an ironmonger," and both gentlemen were subsequently Wardens of their Company. Others, too, were admitted to follow other trades.

Mr. Herbert, the Guildhall Librarian, in his Historical Essay on the City Companies, published fifty years ago, sums up the exactions on the Guilds by the reigning powers in these words:—"Contributions towards setting the poor to work, towards erecting the Royal Exchange, towards cleansing the City ditch, and towards projects of discovering new countries; money for furnishing military and naval armaments; for men, arms, and ammunition to protect the City; for State and City pageants and attendances; for provision of coal and corn, compulsory loans, State lotteries, monopolous patents, concealments, seditious publications and practices, and twenty other sponging expedients were among the more prominent of the engines by which that 'mother of her people,' Elizabeth, and afterwards James and Charles, contrived to screw from the Companies their wealth." And J. P. Malcolm, in the second volume of his "Londinium Redivivum," 1803, when giving his most valuable extracts from the Ironmongers' books (and who speaks of Mr. Sumner, the then clerk of the Guild's "politeness and attention worthy of an enlightened man," and so totally different to some other of the Companies' clerks), remarks "that specie in their hands possessed the faculty of attracting clouds of precepts, and that, if the Company were lavish, the Crown was always ready to receive." Our last chapter proves the case, but a few more entries of another kind will confirm the views expressed.

In 1562 the Ironmongers were called upon to provide without delay nineteen "good appte and talle persones to be souldiers," each of whom was to be provided with "corsletts and weaponed with pykes and billes." This demand meant that if none of the Company's members cared to serve, then they were to find some other men that would, and accordingly liverymen and yeomen had to assist out of their own pockets to meet the charge. Four years later three more soldiers were provided by the Company out of the 100 fully-armed ordered away from the City for service in Ireland;

and, in 1569, no less than twenty-eight "men of honeste behaviour" had to be found "to march against the rebells in the north." A few years later, in 1577, the demand increased, for an order came for 100 "able men, apprentices, journeymen, or others free of the City, of agilitie or honest behaviour," between nineteen and forty years of age, and fully armed, for, says Malcolm in his quaint way, "the noble art of man-killing." The instructions issued out to these "volunteers" are extremely curious to read, for nothing is said in them about evolutions, advancing, retreating, or formation into columns or squares or divisions; and, what is more notable, each man must have been in danger every moment of being blown into the air by his own powder! In 1579 the Ironmongers' proportion of the 3,000 men wanted of the City for the defence of the realm was 110, of which 72 were to be provided with "shott, calvyr, flask, toche, murryn, sword, and dagger, and a pound of powder," and 38 with "pikes, corslett, sword, and daggr." The Armada year of 1588, and the call to arms upon that occasion will be found fully described in the "Historical Essay," printed in 1886; but in 1591, in order to provide the 7,000*l.* required for manning the navy, the Ironmongers lent 344*l.*, having two years previous received notice to have ready 1,920 lbs. of powder. In 1643, when the Committee at Guildhall sent a polite request to Ironmongers' Hall desiring that fifty barrels of gunpowder should be stored there as "a place of safety," the Company politely returned answer that they could not oblige, for not only want of room, but that their tenants next door, having Spaniards, Dutchmen, and Frenchmen lodging in the house, might be placed in danger of no ordinary kind.

In 1596 the Companies were charged with 3,500*l.* for providing twelve ships, two pinnaces, and 1,200 men, and the Ironmongers lent 172*l.* The next demand made for ships or men was in the year 1639, when 1,000*l.* was raised. Readers of history will recollect the case of John Hampden and the "Ship Money" impost, and the Companies' books prove too truly the repeated extortions. The demand on the Ironmongers' for men alone in the forty years previous to 1600 was something like 300, besides their full equipments, and when we reckon the money lent, the powder provided the other calls upon their purse, it will be fully understood that the good old times with this Company were none of the happiest.

We will now mention another branch of the City Companies' "business"—the coal and corn custom. The object was twofold: to supply the poor in times of scarcity at a cheap rate, and to defeat the combinations of dealers. And yet, laudable as the custom was, it is astonishing to find from the results that much imposition was inflicted upon the Companies, and that the demands for storage poured in as fast as the money precepts did. As early as 1605 the Ironmongers agreed "to provide a shipp to fetch sea coles from Newcastle, as other of the twelve Companies intende"; and in 1665 (the Plague year) they laid up 255 chaldrons, all the other Companies laying in quantities in proportion. And here we cannot omit to mention one of the bequests made by a worthy benefactor to the Ironmongers' Company. Margaret Dane, the wife of Alderman William Dane (Sheriff 1569, and twice Master of his Company), by her will, dated in 1579, left in trust to the Company (among other munificent bequests) sufficient money to provide every year 12,000 faggots to be distributed among the poor of each of the twenty-four City Wards, to be used by such poor persons "as fuel to keep them warm." To this day this bequest of three centuries ago is carried out by the company, a certain sum being distributed to each ward. But it will hardly be believed when we state that the opponents to the City Companies have gone out of their way to magnify this praiseworthy bequest into the horrible tale that this good lady left 12,000 faggots yearly to be used for the burning of heretics!

The provision of corn commenced as early as 1521, and continued until the period of the Great Fire in 1666, when, the Companies' mills and granaries being destroyed, the custom ceased, and was not afterwards renewed. In 1579 eight ironmongers were deputed to go to all the City markets and "set the price of meale"; in 1608 the Company was assessed at 88*l.* towards erecting the granaries at Bridewell, and another 88*l.* the following year. Yearly provisioning the markets at Leadenhall, at Queenhithe, and elsewhere continued until 1649, when the Company pleaded that, through being "disabled in their estate," they really were unable to meet the Lord Mayor's demand. A complete summary of this City corn custom will be found in Herbert's "History of the Companies," vol. i., pp. 132-150.

We will mention a few of the "Miscellaneous" precepts which the company were favoured with from time to time. In 1565-66 they subscribed among themselves 100*l.* towards "the building of the new Burse"—the first Royal Exchange. They made loans to Yarmouth (1577), Bury St. Edmunds (1637), and Gloucester (1643) to help those places in their difficulties. They made a benevolence in 1604 of 40*s.* to Messrs. Chandler & Parkhurst, for having procured the passing in Parliament of the Bankruptcy Act, "a matter verie beneficiall to ye comonwealth." In 1631 they agreed to subscribe 20*l.* a year for five years towards the repairing of St. Paul's Cathedral, and again on the rebuilding, after the fire of London, in 1666, they, as individual members, were benefactors. In 1694 they gave 40*s.* to a Greek presbyter of Larissa to help him to get back to his country; in fact, such donations frequently occur in the books. Mr. Nicholl remarks: "Not only are the City Companies called upon to relieve the necessities of private indigence, but there is scarcely any public charity whatever whose petitions for aid are not laid before them."

In the beginning of the reign of James I. (1608-14) the Company, with others, adventured in the New Virginia Plantation Scheme, "to ease the Cittie and suburbs of a swarme of unnecessarie inmates as a continuall cause of dearth and famine, and the verie origenall of all plagues." In 1609 the King offered to the City of London the waste lands in Ulster as another plantation scheme. This, the wisest act of His Majesty, was accepted, and the Ironmongers (among other City Companies) became thus possessed by actual purchase (as shall be shown hereafter) of their Irish estate—the Manor of Lizard. In 1625-27 the Company lent, or advanced, money to the East India Company, and in 1633 to the Greenland Company. It must be mentioned here that, having subscribed to the Virginia Lottery, Captain John Smith subsequently presented to the Company copies of four of his books, all of which, unfortunately, are now missing. As the copies contained dedications (in MS.?) the loss is to be much deplored.

We now turn to more joyful matters—pageantry. The Ironmongers were not behind in any of these. So long ago as 1483 ten of the Company (with proportions from other companies), dressed in murrey-coloured coats, rode to meet the King on his entering the City, and at the subsequent coronation, when the Lord Mayor (Sir Edmund Shaa, goldsmith, and Alderman of Cheap Ward, the same ward over which the present Lord Mayor in 1889 presides) acted as chief butler at the feast, and received from the King and Queen the wine-cups used by them as his fee, Alderman Thomas Breten, Ironmonger, assisted his lordship in his duties. At most of the Royal visits and coronations, and such like festivities, the Company, with others, always had their "standing" and precedency, and in this respect the "place" was much contested. A proof occurs in the history of the dispute between the Skinners and Merchant Taylors in 1484. Upon appeal to the Lord Mayor "for norishing of peas and love," he decreed that from henceforth the Skinners should dine with the Merchant Taylors at their hall one year, and the Merchant Taylors at Skinners' Hall the next year, and so yearly alternately for ever should each company have precedence. And for 400 years has this most excellent decree been celebrated yearly, each Company toasting in the other's hall their "root and branch," and wishing them "to flourish for ever."

In 1541, when Queen Anne Bullen came from Greenwich by water to Westminster, the Company of Ironmongers spent no less than 9*l.* on the festivity. Their barge cost 26*s.* 8*d.*, and their provisions included gurnets, fresh salmon, eels, bread and cheese, wine, claret, and a kilderkin of ale. A reference to Nichols's "London Pageants," or his "Progresses" of Queen Elizabeth and James I., will tell in full the interesting character of these City shows, and the gorgeous displays made by the citizens, who then, as now, never were niggardly in their tokens of welcome. One of the most curious of these outdoor scenes was "the setting of the marching watch," when 2,000 persons, apparelled in holiday costume, with 700 lighted cressets, borne aloft, paraded the City. A description of a visit by Henry VIII., dressed in the costume of one of his own guards, will be found in the first volume of Knight's "London." The last entry in the Ironmongers' books is dated 1567, but an account of expenses a quarter of a century earlier shows that 800 cresset lights cost 2*s.* 4*d.* per 100; a dozen straw hats, 12*d.*; armourer, 6*s.* The Company's banquet cost 36*s.* Among the items of the feast were: A peece of beef, 4*d.*; a breast of veel, 7*d.*; a neck and breast of mutton, 6*d.*; a goose, 9*d.*; four rabbits, 1*s.*; bread, 6*d.*; butter, 1½*d.*; water, 1*d.* The cook and two assistants, 7*d.*; six gallons of wine, 7*s.*; and a gallon of ale, 2*d.*

Lord Mayor's Day and the Lord Mayor's Show was another City festival red letter day from early times. Until the year 1752, when the Act for altering the calendar came into force, the presentation of the Lord Mayor took place on October 29, but since that year it has been November 9. Sir John Norman, "Draper," in 1452, was the first chief magistrate to go to Westminster by water; Lord Mayor Finnis, in 1856, the last. Most of the Lord Mayors have had their shows, the pageantry at which has been most elaborate, especially during the seventeenth century. The following is a complete list of the "Ironmonger" Lord Mayors:—

1409-10 } 1417-18 }	Sir Richard Marlow
1442-43	Sir John Hatherley
1566-67	Sir Christopher Draper
1569-70	Sir Alexander Avenon
1581-82	Sir James Harvey
1592-93	Sir William Rowe
1609-10	Sir Thomas Cambell
1618-19	Sir Sebastian Harvey
1629-30	Sir James Cambell
1635-36	Sir Christopher Cletherow
1685-86	Sir Robert Geffery
1714-15	Sir William Humfreys, Bart.
1719-20	Sir George Thorold, Bart.
1741-42	Sir Robert Godschall (who died in his mayoralty on June 26, 1742)
1749-50	Sir Samuel Pennant (who died in his mayoralty on May 20, 1750)
1751-52	Robert Alsop (elected upon the death of Thomas Winterbottom, June 4, 1751)
1762-63 } 1769-70 }	William Beckford (died June 21, 1770; see his monument in Guildhall)
1802-03	Sir Charles Price, Bart.
1810-11	J. J. Smith, Esq. (Lord Nelson's executor)
1828-29	William Thompson, Esq.

As we have already stated, some of the early Lord Mayor's Shows were elaborate, and illustrative of the Company's trade name. They will be found chronicled in Nichols's "Pageants" and in Fairholt's "Lord Mayor's Day Pageants" (Percy Society, 1843-45). The Guildhall Banquet tickets during the past 100 years have been exceedingly interesting as specimens of design and printing, the early ones being by Bartolozzi and his school. A nearly complete set is in our own collection, those at Guildhall, strangely enough, only dating back some fifty years, the reason being that the show and banquet has always been the private and personal festival of the Lord Mayor and two Sheriffs, the former paying a moiety of the expenses, the total generally ranging from 2,000*l*. to 3,000*l*. It is, therefore, a vulgar error to suppose that the Citizens and ratepayers are taxed a penny.

The earliest notice of the Pageantry in the Ironmongers' books is 1566, but the most complete account is that at the inauguration of Sir James Cambell, 1629, which was compiled by Thomas Dekker, and entitled "London's Tempe." It cost the Company 180*l*. There were six elaborately "got up" pageants representing: for the water a sea lion and two sea horses, and for the land an estridge, Lemnion's Forge, Tempe, or the Field of Hapines, and Apollo's Palace representing the seven liberal sciences. The fourth or trade pageant is worth quoting. It is described as "The Lemnion Forge." In it are Vulcan the Smith of Lemnos, with his servants (the Cyclopes), whose names are Pyracmon, Brontes, and Sceropes, working at the anvile. "Their habite are wastcoates and leather aprons, their hair black and shaggy, in knotted curles. A fire is seene in the forge, bellowes blowing, some filing, some at other workes; thunder and lightning on occasion. As the smithes are at worke they singe in praise of iron, the anvile, and hammer, by the concordant stroakes and soundes of which Tuball Cayne became the first inventor of musicke."

Brave iron ! brave hammer ! from your sound
The art of Musicke has her ground ;
On the anvile thou keep'st time,
Thy knick-a-knock is a smithes best chyme.

In proper places sit Cupid and Jove, Vulcan and Jove alternately singing praises, the song ending thus :—

Brave Iron ! what praise
Deserves it ! more tis beate more it obeyes ;
The more it suffers, more it smoothes offence ;
In drudgery it shines with patience.
This fellowshipp was then with judging eyes
United to the Twelve great Companies :
It being farre more worthy than to fill
A file inferiour. You's the Sun's guilt hill ;
On to'ot ! Love guardes you on ! Cyclopes, a ring
Make with your hammers, to whose musicke sing

CHAPTER VI.

FOUR HUNDRED YEARS OF THE IRONMONGERS' HISTORY.—III.

THE Lord Mayor's Show of the olden time, unlike the annual carnival of the latter half of the nineteenth century, was in reality illustrative of the trade to which (by Company) the chief magistrate belonged, and notwithstanding the prejudices against pageantry at the present time, we are staunch advocates for some annual popular display whereby the rising generation of our great City may, like the apprentices of old London, have visible proof that the Lord Mayor is a reality and not invisible to his subjects, and that if they will only put their shoulder to the wheel and emulate Hogarth's industrious apprentice they in time stand the best chance of living in a big house, riding in a gilt coach, and wearing that big gold chain which yearly makes their appetites so keen and their eyes glisten with delight.

These Lord Mayor pageants of the seventeenth century were, as we have stated, partly a show on the Thames and partly a show in the City streets. Designed by the City poet of the period, the descriptions were usually printed in a small volume and circulated among the Lord Mayor's friends and the members of the company. Probably the largest volume on the subject is the reprint of the Fishmongers' pageant of 1616, edited by J. G. Nichols in 1844, a large folio with twelve illustrations, *facsimiles* of the original drawings. Our own copy of this work belonged to Mr. Recorder Gurney, and has the plates beautifully hand-painted and illuminated. And the smallest book upon so great a subject is a 32-paged duodecimo entitled "The Lord Mayor of London: a Sketch of the Origin, History, and Antiquity of the Office," printed in 1860, and containing, as we believe, every fact to that date worth knowing about the office.

There are two items in connection with the 1629 show which must not be omitted. That "gentle angler," Izaak Walton, a City apprentice who had been admitted a member of the Ironmongers' Company eleven years before, on November 12, 1618, was one of the thirty-two members of the yeomanry who took part in the pageant. The "Sea Lion" and the "Estridge," after the day's ceremony was over, were brought in state to Ironmongers' Hall, "to be sett upp for the Company's use." We do not know how long the lion remained so proudly exalted, but certainly not so long as the world-renowned relic still called the "original" dagger with which "brave Walworth knight Wat Tyler slew" in 1381, and which, after being carried in many a Fishmongers' pageant, rests at the present time in a glass case in Fishmongers' Hall. The carved-wood ostrich still exists.

The same year that Walton was admitted to the freedom (1618) the Ironmongers' pageant, exhibited a few days previous, and at which, of course, he was unable to be a

D 2

THE HEARSE-CLOTH, OR IRONMONGERS' FUNERAL PALL, 1515.—PLATE I.

"The Blessed Virgin Mary in Glory."

(See page 55.)

representative member, was devised by Anthony Munday. There were three special attractions — an ironmine, an ostrich (which eats brass and iron to help its digestion !), and a leopard, the latter a compliment to the Lord Mayor, whose arms bore three leopards' heads, and whose crest was a leopard. The cost of these was 103*l.* Some of the payments are curious to read :—Six green (wood) men, with four assistants, who threw up fireworks as they marched along, cost 8*l.* 10*s.*; two men-of-war ships cost 30*l.*; 120 chambers or small cannon, 34*l.*, with "4 lbs. of almond comfits put in the bullets in the cannon," 4*s.*; banners and streamers, 36*l.*; "a new antient staff with faire guilt head," 6*s.* 8*d.*; thirty-two trumpeters, 29*l.*; taffety sarsnet, cloth, fringe, &c., 45*l.*; "meat for the children's breakfast," 42*s.*; and marshalling the show, 3*l.* 6*s.* 8*d.* Last, but not least, there was such a gigantic operation performed that it reads like a Chicago event of to-day—"Removing the iron myne to the hall, 2*s.* 8*d.*"! The next Ironmongers' trade pageant (1635) cost 180*l.*

The last Lord Mayor's Show of the seventeenth century which the Ironmongers specially connected themselves with was that of Sir Robert Geffery in 1685, and who subsequently proved himself "a worthy benefactor" to the Company and the founder of their almshouses. It was designed by Matthew Taubman, and cost 473*l.* In his opening speech the author reminds us :—

"Though poets place the Iron Age the last, it had certainly a being and was of use before silver or gold had a value among the ancients. To calculate the original founders we must go further than Tubal Cain; nor is it probable the first Cain built such a vast city without materials and instruments proper for so great a design in opening the quarries and diving into the stony bowels of the earth. As the mystery of iron-working is most ancient, so is it most useful to the State, and most profitable to the merchant and artificer. Iron, for the universality of its use, may be called the efficient matter of all other mysteries, being either an ingredient or necessary instrument in all arts and professions. Take away the use of iron, all trading must cease."

Taubman devised this "London's Annual Triumph," as he called it, in four pageants. The first exhibited a pyramid, on which was placed the Company's founder, King Edward the Fourth, with Victory associated with Vigilance, Courage, and Conduct, and those four beautiful virgins, Triumph, Honour, Peace, and Plenty; the second pageant was a sea chariot; the third, a triumphal arch of loyalty, upon which was exalted Fame, supported by Truth, Union, and Concord; the fourth (or trade) pageant represented the Mountain of Ætna casting forth its sulphurous matter, with Vulcan, hammer in hand, at his anvil, attended by three Cyclops, also at anvils, answering Brontes, Steropes, and Pyracmon, who were forging thunderbolts for Jove and heads of arrows for Cupid. Amidst all the din of music and noise of the smiths were to be seen attendants throwing up ore from an ironmine, at the entrance to which stood Polypheme, a great giant, with only one eye, and that in the middle of his forehead, who, with a huge iron bar in one hand and a sword in the other, kept guard "to prevent all others but the Right Worshipful the Company of Ironmongers (whose peculiar prerogative it is) to enter." Every figure in the pageant acted well his part, and Vulcan and Apollo probably took the lead, for Vulcan, addressing the Lord Mayor, sang:—

> Here, sir, in iron mines of sulphurous earth,
> Where smoak and fiery vapours take their birth,
> We forge out thunderbolts for incensed Jove,
> And heads of arrows for the God of Love.

Victory declaring:—

> Against cold ir'n no armour can prevail;
> There's no resistance in a coat of male.

At the subsequent Guildhall banquet was sung the Company's song in praise of iron, and this was followed by another specially prepared to greet the King (James the Second), who was present.

It was nothing out of the way in those times for Royalty to dine with the citizens, with whom both kings and queens were "hale fellows well met." The State papers and the Royal letters prove to the hilt that in a great many instances the citizens would have preferred their room to their company. The best anecdote belongs to the "merry monarch" Charles II., who, dining at Guildhall, so "hobnob'd" with the Lord Mayor that they did not know "the other from which." The King, however, managed to leave without ceremony, and was just getting into his coach in Guildhall Yard when my Lord Mayor, discovering his loss, overtook him, and begged "Mr. King" to return and "take t'other bottle," which, no doubt, he did, not forgetting a few days later to send to my lord his little bill for the usual loan!

In recent years the City Companies have taken up the question of technical education, and it cannot be denied that in many instances they have excelled themselves in this most praiseworthy work. If any reform is wanted, both Royalty and Government are the last to do it, but with the City Guilds, notwithstanding what is said against them, they have been found to the fore when anything beneficial to the people is required to be carried out, although in many instances they have neither been compelled to do it nor has it been beneficial to themselves in particular. From time to time the Companies had subscribed largely to the charities, &c., of societies not always of their special trade; but in January, 1860, the Painters' Stainers' Company took the lead in quite another direction by giving notice that in June following they would hold an exhibition of decorative works at their Hall in Little Trinity Lane, Cannon Street. There were thirty-five exhibitors, and this, the first exhibition of its kind, proving eminently successful, was held again the following year, and has been repeated upon many occasions since. The next Company's announcement was that of the Ironmongers, who held a conversazione and exhibition of iron-work and curiosities in May, 1861, and, although this was not a trade exhibition, but promoted by the London and Middlesex Archæological Society, yet it brought together such a remarkable collection as had never before been seen in a City Company's hall. In proof of this there is in print a very scarce volume entitled "A Catalogue of the Antiquities and Works of Art Exhibited at Ironmongers' Hall, London, in the Month of May, 1861," edited by the well-known Shakesperian scholar, the late G. R. French, at that time surveyor to the Company. So laborious was the editing of this ponderous volume, of 642 large quarto pages—for Mr. French was compelled at last to rely on his own resources in order to complete the book—that it was not issued until August, 1869. The actual cost of the book will never be known, for Mr. French died in October, 1881, and all the remaining copies, the drawings, the wood blocks of the 331 illustrations, and a large quantity of the original MSS. relating to the exhibition, the book, &c., had been already dispersed. The "Catalogue," however, will keep his memory before the public long after everything else will have passed away. In this volume will be found described and illustrated, not only the charters, the plate, and other curiosities belonging to the Ironmongers, but also those belonging to other corporations, and the principal owners of iron and other antiquities and curios.

As we have said, the exhibition was opened in May, 1861. Over 600 persons attended the private view on Wednesday the 8th, 420 were present on the 9th, 1,345 on the 10th, and 1,678 on the 11th and last day—in all, more than 4,000 persons, each of whom on entering signed his or her name in a book still preserved by the Company. On the fourth day the Prince Consort attended, and he signed his name in the Court book. It was the regret of every one that, owing to the immense value of the antiquities, &c., the exhibition could not be kept open longer. Since 1861 the Ironmongers have had several other interesting meetings, and at the end of the month of March, 1889, the Blacksmiths, by special permission, held its first trade exhibition in the same building, following, as they do in this laudable work, the Fishmongers', Plumbers', Fanmakers', Turners', Carpenters', Shipwrights', Horners', Coachmakers', and other City Guilds.

A most important step was taken in 1872, when the Ironmongers joined the other City Guilds in the promotion of technical education. Mr. Henry Grissell, an old ironmaster and then senior warden, represented the Company at the meetings. Speaking of this great movement, the report of the City Livery Companies' Commission in 1884 tells us:—"The subject of technical education has within the last few years been taken up by the Companies. The Clothworkers' Company has promoted the establishment of Yorkshire College at Leeds, where instruction is given in the manufacture of woollen goods, and similar institutions at Bradford, Huddersfield, and other places, the present seats of its former trade. The City and Guilds of London Institute for the Advancement of Technical Education has also recently been formed. It is an association consisting of representatives of the City of London, and of most of the more considerable Livery Companies, and the funds which have been placed at its disposal by the City and the Companies are very large. A building fund of upwards of 100,000*l.* has been contributed, and annual subscriptions have been promised amounting to about 25,000*l.* a year. The former sum has been, or is being, expended on a technical college in Finsbury and a central institution in South Kensington." When we state that the technical education scheme is likely to cost the companies 50,000*l.* a year, no one should say a word against them, but rather applaud the City for having inaugurated a grand work without Government aid or the support of the great employers of labour in outer London.

The attacks made in Parliament during the past quarter of a century against the City Companies have so far fallen back with a crushing defeat upon the enemy. Mr. Maguire's Irish spoliation scheme of 1868 and 1869 ended, as it was expected it would, in proving then (as now) that there are many worse-managed estates there than those belonging to the City Guilds. In 1876 and 1877 Mr. James distinguished himself by also attacking the Companies, and upon three occasions had the majority of the House against his spoliation designs. Then, again, the "Royal Commission" of 1880 has enabled our descendants to possess the finest collection of historical details relating to the Companies it is possible to get together, and for that alone—not for having obtained the information at so serious an outlay to the Companies and the public purse—historical students are truly thankful.

We will now say a few words about the livery and the yeomanry, or freemen generally, which, unlike any other City Company, form the only two grades of membership in the Ironmongers (all the livery forming the court); and this exception, together with the rarity of the oldest yeoman being considered eligible for the "Clothing," makes this Company in every particular as regards the term Livery Company unique. We are very sorry it is so, because there are many of the freemen who are not only eligible by time service, but are in many other ways equally eligible by their devoted interest and their ability; while the peculiar order of the Guild prevents them being members of other Companies where their services, &c., would be more appreciated.

The Livery.—The introduction of liveries into the City Companies took place 600 years ago. The chief members wore a gown or cloak with hood, and for distinction sake each Company had its own colours; but we cannot learn what the Ironmongers' were. Edward IV.'s charter is directed to "all the freemen of the mystery and art of Ironmongers," and appoints "one master and two keepers or wardens, and the commonalty" and their successors to have perpetual succession, with powers to frame ordinances, &c. The ordinances of 1498 (in which the warden was made responsible in selecting the necessary cloth at the drapers) were revised in the reign of Elizabeth, and finally approved, as stated in our fourth chapter, in February, 1581. Four quarterly courts were to be held, at which the livery called "the Clothing" were to pay their quarterage, and those neglecting to attend were to be fined 2*s.* And at these courts the yeomanry were to appear and also pay their quarterage. And upon the admittance of a member of the yeomanry to the livery he was to pay 6*s.* 8*d.* upon receiving "his pattern of his lyverie." Those not paying fines to be sent to prison. There does not appear to be a record officially fixing the strength of the livery. The earliest complete list is dated 1537, when it appears that the number was 59, at the head being William Denham (Alderman) and Thomas Lewen (Sheriff of London). In 1570 there were 54 liverymen. In 1687, before the restoration patent of James II., the list comprised a master, 2 wardens, 44 assistants, and 16 liverymen—in all 60, or one more than in the list just 150 years previous. In 1710 the list was 95, but in 1776 the court had increased to 100. In 1801 there were 97 all told; in 1828, 85; in 1833 again 98; in 1847, 82; in 1857, 99; in 1867, 84; since which time there has been a gradual decrease, the total numbering only 48 last year. Now this is an extraordinary decline, and we should not have collected all these numbers had it not been that for some years past the yeomanry, among whom are many worthy and representative men, have been discussing their chance of obtaining "the clothing," seeing that "calls" to the court are by no means regular, and when they do take place younger men, generally sons or relatives of thosealready on the court, are chosen over the heads of "antient" yeomen equally capable, and certainly more so by long connection with the Company, of looking after its interests, their position in the commercial world being a guarantee that they would serve their brethren without the "fee or reward" about which the Royal Commission on the Companies had so much to say. The ancient dress or costume of a liveryman in his cap and furred robe is shown in the Leathersellers' charter facsimiles in the magnificent quarto work on that Guild, edited by the late W. H. Black, for the Company in 1871. From time to time many ordinances were made about the citizens' dress, special reprimands to the livery being administered in 1619 and 1677 for not appearing in their gowns; and in 1698 the Corporation issued an order that in future no one should join as a liveryman one of the twelve Companies unless he had an estate of 1,000*l.*, or one of the minor Guilds under 500*l.* By an order passed in 1790 no servant is eligible for election on the livery. In 1627 a very curious dispute arose between Humphrey Hook, then residing at Bristol, where he had served municipal offices, and the court, they calling upon him to be their warden, he having been a freeman twenty-four years. The Company appears to have won the case.

The Yeomanry are the freemen of the Company generally, and about 300 in number. Although not of the "Clothing" (livery) a yeoman was described by an authority in 1759 as being of military origin, and in many respects equal to an esquire, the former fighting with arrows and bows made of yew tree, the latter carrying for distinction and defence a shield. In the ordinances of 1581 it was laid down that the yeomany should pay their quarterage of 4*d.* a quarter, and that the wardens of the livery should, when necessary, help the "wardens of the yeomanry"; the four quarter-days are specially named as July 25, or St. James' day, October 18, being St. Luke's day, New Year's day, and the Wednesday in Easter week, on which last-named day the new warden of the yeomanry should be elected for two years, there having been two wardens allowed by petition in 1497. All members failing to appear on these days were fined. It was also decreed that two suppers should be kept yearly at the hall, for which the wardens were allowed 33*s.* 4*d.* Mr. Nicholl, the Company's historian, states that the wardens of the yeomanry stand in the same position to their body as the wardens of the livery do; but of late years, their duties having declined, only one warden now represents the freemen. The quarterage, too, of 16*d.* per annum has for many years past ceased to be collected, and the two meetings and suppers at the hall, which formerly took place on election day and St. Luke's day (by and under the authority of the ancient ordinances of 1581, confirmed by the Lord Chancellor in 1590, assisted by the will in 1653 of "a worthy benefactor," none other than the clerk of the Company, Ralph Handson, and finally approved by the Charity Trustees in 1876), were in the year 1830 discontinued, and two dinners appointed to take place at the hall in their stead. At these meetings and festivals, which are proved to be no unimportant rights, the senior warden of the livery presides, drinking health and prosperity to the yeomanry "root and branch, and may they flourish for ever"; their warden replying, and desiring his brethren in return to drink to the health of the senior warden. These are the only occasions when the members have the opportunity and pleasure of meeting in a body, and may the ancient custom—which by special ordinances became the freemen's right—long continue is a wish echoed by the whole Company. Formerly the bread and cheese and ale repast was obtained from the old King's Head Tavern opposite the hall in Fenchurch Street, and it was within the walls of the New London Tavern, erected on its site, that the warden of the yeomanry for the year 1888 held the St. Luke's day meeting, and by discoursing to his brethren upon the history and antiquity of the Company, and exhibiting a number of curiosities relating to the Ironmongers, not only brought together a most enthusiastic audience, but for the first time in the recollection of the yeomanry made them feel interested in their Guild, and to pass a resolution never to permit the opportunity of meeting twice a year (by virtue of the old ordinance) to lapse in the future.

The freedom of the Ironmongers' Company is obtainable by patrimony (as children of freemen, for there have been free women admitted), servitude (as apprentices to freemen), and redemption (by payment of one hundred guineas, or honorary presentation); but, curious to relate, although there are members of the Company "learned in the law" at the present time (as freemen by patrimony), no attorney is eligible for election by redemption. By ordinance dated 1657 no person is to change the copy of his freedom, and by an order of Court made November 21, 1878, "no person who is free of any other Company can be admitted to the freedom of the Ironmongers' Company, nor can he become free of another Company after being admitted to the freedom of this Company." This order necessarily makes the Ironmongers a select body corporate, and unlike the other Companies of the City. Upon being elected freeman the member makes a declaration accordingly, and when elected warden he takes the warden's oath to look after the Company's welfare during his term of office. The beadle of the Company half-yearly sends out the notices: "You are desired by the warden of the yeomanry to meet at Ironmongers' Hall" (on the day of election, or St. Luke's) "when a court will be holden in the usual manner." At this court the warden presides and signs the freemen's book, as do also such members who may be present. The beadle, having previously written to those of the yeomanry eligible for office of warden, submits the replies to the court. The election is entirely by their own vote, and selected from those present; and we believe for the first time in 1881, when Mr. F. W. Pellatt was chosen. The warden of the following year (Mr. Alfred Marshall, C.E.) was re-elected in 1883, he having taken an active part in the freemen's interest; and at the election in 1888 (the Armada Tercentenary celebration year) the warden chosen was the author of the "Historical Essay" upon the Spanish Armada, who, being a member of the Plymouth and London committees, was selected in commemoration of the Company's zeal at the time of the threatened invasion 300 years previous. At the yeomanry meeting at Easter, 1883, a special vote of condolence with the family was recorded in the minute-book upon the decease of "its much respected clerk, Simon Adams Beck, Esq., who for the long period of nearly fifty years so ably discharged the duties of his very important office." The death of Mr. Beck, who was at one time Governor of the Gas Light and Coke Company—the district in which the works are situated being now known as Beckton—was a sad loss to every member of the Ironmongers' Company. His portrait appropriately hangs close to that of Mr. John Nicholl, the Company's historian, in the court-room at the hall.

CHAPTER VII.

THE APPRENTICES, THE HALL, AND THE IRISH ESTATE.

THE London apprentice of the olden time was as different a personage to the 'prentice lad of to-day as the streets of the City are now unlike the thoroughfares of two or three centuries ago. The ancient Guild ordinances relating to apprentices prove that they were considered a most important part of the establishment of a citizen, and this is not to be wondered at when we consider that not only the trade of his master, but the trade of London, depended entirely upon the skilled artisan and craftsman's ability, without which all the money-bags of the merchant were of little use. We could fill a volume with the history and anecdotes of the apprentice, but must content ourselves by giving a brief summary only; and the notes that we do give will show that our apprentices were not unworthy of the City, notwithstanding they were never backward in crying "Clubs! clubs!" and eager for the fray. In every festival, on the "high days and holidays" of civic life, at the marching watch or a Lord Mayor's Show, at "going a Maying" to Shooters' Hill, and archery practice in Finsbury Fields, the apprentice was an expected visitant. As he existed in the days of James I., Sir Walter Scott, in his "Fortunes of Nigel," conveys to us a presentable and true picture.

Since the year 1662, no sooner was a boy aged fourteen than a master was found, and to him he was "bound" to serve, to follow his master's trade, and to learn it until the age of twenty-one, when, having proved a good apprentice, he was admitted to the freedom of the Company to which such master belonged. Sometimes his master in the meantime died, and that necessitated his being "turned over" to another employer. If the boy misbehaved himself, then the Company and the Chamberlain took him in hand, and, if incorrigible, to Bridewell he was sent. It neither benefited the Corporation, the Company, nor the master to take too severe measures, and in recent years the cases have been few where correction has been administered, although to our minds it should have been oftener; and instances, too, have occurred where the master ought to have paid the penalty as well.

The earliest enrolment of a City apprentice was in the reign of Edward II., or five centuries and a half ago. There is a curious case recorded in the Guildhall Letter-book H, folio 42, of the year 1376, when William Grendone, *alias* Credelle, a scrivener, was sent to Newgate and fined for making a false indenture between William Ayllesham, a goldsmith, and Nicholas, the son of William Flourman. The indenture was for nine years, and the surety, instead of the father of the boy, was named as "the Cross at the North

ST. ELIZABETH.

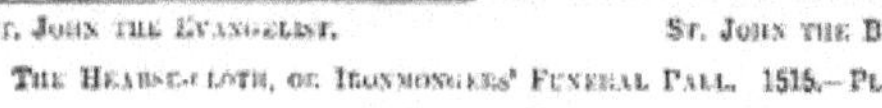

ST. JOHN THE EVANGELIST. ST. JOHN THE BAPTIST.

THE HEARSE-CLOTH, OR IRONMONGERS' FUNERAL PALL. 1515.—PLATE II.

(See page 55.)

Door." This cross—Broken Cross, or the Stone Cross—was at the north door of St. Paul's, and, having been erected in the reign of Henry III., remained there until 1390, and in those superstitious ages any transaction there was, as a rule, considered binding. Each cross in the City had certain stalls, or stands, or stations, and these from time to time were let to persons who thus became Stationers, and in course of time left these stations at the Cross, and took up their position in and about Paternoster Row.

The Ironmongers' ordinance for the year 1498 (confirmed by the Judges February 16, 1581) specially mentions the apprentice, as we have shown in our fourth chapter. The housing, the clothing, and the general welfare of the boy were fully set down, even to the command that the master "shall not suffre his (the apprentice's) here to growe to long!" Again, "Every maister is sworne at the Guyldehall to make his prentice free wthout any cost or charge to the prentice"—a custom, we regret to say, long ago forgotten; and a century and a half after the making of the ordinance it was further ordered that any master putting in an appearance with the boy at the hall "before he have orderly cutt and barbed his hayre to the liking of the Mr and Wardens of the Company" was to be fined twenty shillings. One of the best City ordinances was that preventing the early marrying of artisans, in 1556—a custom which had produced "povertie, penurie, and lacke of livyng." The Act recites:—

> That by reason of the over hastie marriges and over sone setting up of housholdes of and by the youth and young folkes of the sayde citie wch hath comonly used and yet do, to marry themselves as sone as ever thay come oute of theyr apprenticehode be thaye never so young and unskilful, yea and often tymes many of them so poore that they scantly have of theire proper goodeyes wherewith to baye theire marriage apparel, and to furnish ther houses with implements and other thinges necessary for the exercise of ther occupacons whereby they should be able to sustayne themselves and theire family;

therefore, for the remedy it was ordered that all apprentices in future should not be made free until the age of twenty-four, at which age his apprenticeship is to expire, and any master violating the order to pay a fine of 20*l*. It is a curious coincidence, too, that in the original rules, dated September, 1557, for the government of "the House of Bridewell," which hospital the City had recently obtained from Edward VI., there is a special ordinance relating to the oversight of "the Nail House":—

> Now for the setting on work of the idle; it shall be very requisite that with as much speed, and as conveniently as ye may, that ye increase the number of apprentices being taught in the said faculty and discharge the number of journeymen, to the intent the same apprentices being themselves perfect and absolute therein may train and teach such of our poor children or other needy people as hereafter we shall call out of the hateful life of idleness.

As already stated, the overseers, artmasters, taskmasters, workmasters, or artificers, for the foremen of the Bridewell shops, where the boys were taught clothworking, weaving, pinmaking, &c., were so called, had under their charge sometimes 150, and as many as 250. Two of the hospital minute entries tell us:—

> 1602, Oct. 21.—Richard Brookes, fustian weaver, engages to take during seven years next ensuing 40 vagrant boyes and wenches of this city as

apprentices to keep in diett, apparell, washing and wringing: the said R. Brookes to receive with every of the said children at their coming clean apparell and 10*l.* yearly.

1604, February 20.—Francis Ackland, pinmaker, engages to take 40 vagrant boys as apprentices.

And in 1606 the minute-book reports the order that the names of all proposed apprentices brought into the House of Bridewell shall be registered, as also the master's name. During the last century the apprentices in the house gradually declined, for in 1708 there were 140, in 1768 only 60, in 1789 only 36, and in 1791 only 26, illustrating but too forcibly the change in the times. It is probably not generally known that in the olden time the Bridewell boys upon the ringing of the fire-bell by the beadle used to drop their tools and start off to the fire, wherever it was situate in the metropolis. The result was :—

They were active, to be sure, and serviceable; but what were the consequences to themselves? They were thrown among all those profligates which a fire collects in the streets. They got liquor, they got money, and frequently roamed about the town all night without controul. The masters lost the benefit of the next day's labour; and not seldom boys were hurt, and for a long time disabled from working. It is about 20 years since this very pernicious practice was restrained.

By the above quotations, written in 1798, we have shown that Bridewell was not only a House of Correction for City vagrants, but was from its foundation a real workhouse and artisans' workshop. Many ignorant and misinformed persons have before now gone out of their way to abuse this institution, and declare that it never was put to the use the royal founder intended. We could multiply our proofs that Bridewell always was a useful house until Government, more than a century ago, meddled with the City management, and spoilt this and Christ's Hospital as well.

Another ancient ordinance of the City is dated 1582, when every freeman was charged to take such steps necessary to prevent, and not to suffer under any circumstances, "servants, apprentices, journemen, or children, to repare or goe to annye playes, peices or enterludes, either wi^th^n the Citie or suburbs," under the severe pains and penalties "at the discretion of me and my brethren." Exactly a century later, on August 9, 1682, some 2,000 apprentices of London, who had taken active steps in the address to Charles II. for the support of the institution, were feasted in Merchant Taylors' Hall, the king specially sending them two fat bucks for the occasion.

The following is a copy of an original apprenticeship indenture, dated 1676. It is printed on vellum, 7 by 4 inches in size, the names and date being the only portions written :—

THIS INDENTURE Witnesseth that Clement Aleyn, Sonn of Clement Aleyn, of Welton, in the County of Northampton, Gentleman, doth put himself Apprentice to Samuell Clerke, Citizen and IRONMONGER of London, to learn his Art: and with him (after the manner of an Apprentice) to serve from the day of the date hereof unto the full end and term of Seaven Years from thence next following to be fully complete and ended. During which term the said Apprentice his said Master shall faithfully serve, his secrets keep, his lawful commandments everywhere gladly do. He shall do no damage to his said Master, nor see to be done of others, but that he to his power shall let or forthwith give warning to his said Master of the same. He shall not waste the goods of his said Master, nor lend them unlawfully to any. He shall not commit fornication nor contract matrimony within the said term. He shall not play at Cards, Dice, Tables, or any other unlawful Games, whereby his said Master may have any loss with his own goods or others during the said term without license of his said Master, he shall neither buy nor sell. He shall not haunt Taverns or Playhouses, nor absent himself from his said Master's service day or night unlawfully. But in all things as a faithful Apprentice he shall behave himself towards his said Master and all his during the said term. And the said Master his said Apprentice in the same Art which he useth by the best means that he can, shall teach and instruct, or cause to be taught and instructed, finding unto his said Apprentice meat, drink, apparel, lodging, and all other necessaries, according to the custom of the City of London during the said term. And for the true performance of all and every the said Covenants and Agreements either of the said parties bindeth himself unto the other by these presents. In witness whereof the parties above named to these Indentures interchangeably have put their hands and Seals the Three and Twentieth day of Maye, Anno Dom. 1676, and in the xxviiith Year of the Reign of our Sovereign Lord King Charles the Second over England, &c.

CLEMENT ALEYN.

Sealed and dd. in the pres. of Tho. Heatly, Clerke.

By the Act of Common Council, passed March, 1889, apprentices can now be bound for four years instead of seven, and instead of the master being compelled (as of old) to make the apprentice an indoor servant, he is to pay wages sufficient to keep the boy in food, clothing, &c., elsewhere, as may be arranged. This term of four years also entitles the apprentice to his freedom if the bindings are to citizens, and effected by the Chamberlain and the Companies. The Ironmongers so long ago as January, 1863, had (when desired) adopted the five years' term, but then, while it gave the boy the Company's freedom, it did not confer that of the City. Thus, at last, in this official four years' term, we have arrived at a most satisfactory settlement of a long and often heartburning grievance.

The Ironmongers' Hall, where the bindings take place and the Company's business transacted, is situated in Fenchurch Street, one house westward of Billiter Street. The original ground upon which the premises stand was purchased by nineteen ironmongers, members of the ancient Guild, in October, 1457, and the original purchase deeds still exist to prove that the site is the private property of the descendants of those nineteen brethren of the Guild—if there is really any law extant that freehold property belongs to the "root and branch" of a true-born Englishman. The Hall is mentioned in 1479 as being in the parish of All Hallows Staining, in the Ward of Aldgate. Between the parochial authorities and the Company long existed a dispute upon the burning question of tithes, until some twenty years ago it reached the crisis. A warrant was issued, and four of the candelabra and two of the loving cups were "in a friendly way," in order to test the case, placed on a table in the Hall and momentarily seized by the official, and as quickly restored upon the usual bonds being given for the superior Court's decision. A few years before—in 1862—some beautiful specimens of ornamental ironwork, which the company had erected in the Corporation pew in the church as rests for the sword and mace, suddenly disappeared, but upon question raised as suddenly returned. There is a funny entry in the churchwardens' accounts of this parish for the year 1494: "Payd for a kylcherkyn of good ale, which was drunkyn in the Yrynmongers' Hall, all chargis born xij*s.* ij*d.*" We should like to know what brought about this merry-making 400 years ago. Could it have been "a parochial settlement" of the dispute of 1479?

In Aggas's map of the City, of the reign of Elizabeth, Ironmongers' Hall is depicted as a range of buildings (among which was the clerk's residence). There was no entrance from Fenchurch Street, but only through a long garden having entry from Leadenhall Street. That there was a garden to the Hall is certain, because in the records, about the year 1540, there are numerous interesting entries similar to these:—

ffor a gardener ffor a daye and a ballffe ffor cuttyng of
vynes and dressing of rosses .. .. xij*d.*
to a gardener for V dayes worke .. .. iij*s.* iiij*d.*
ffor cutting of the knotts of ye rosemarie in the garden x*d.*

The first Hall remained until 1585, when, being found "ruinous and in greate decay," it was rebuilt, and a kitchen erected. The cost was large—something like 600*l.*—but the ground covered was somewhat extensive. Tapestry was ordered for the Hall in 1590, and in 1629 further additions were made. In 1686 new sundials were erected, and in 1701 a new wall was put up to prevent the persons in the tavern next door looking across the Company's garden into the private apartments of the Company. In 1707 a mulberry tree was planted in the garden, and in 1719 some new lime trees, so that the Ironmongers' garden was quite a rural retreat, and like the Drapers' garden, which has only of late years been covered over by bricks and mortar.

The second Ironmongers' Hall was not burnt in the great fire of 1666, although it was surrounded by the destructive demon. A certain William Christmas, shipwright, did some good service to the Company upon the occasion, so that in March, 1667, he received a gratuity. In 1677 the Corporation ordered all public buildings to keep leather buckets, hand-squirts, &c., to be ready in case of fire, and the Ironmongers provided themselves with thirty buckets, one engine, six pickaxes, three ladders, and two squirts, the latter being of brass, 3 feet long and 9 inches diameter. To this day may be seen some, if not the, buckets, hanging in the vestibule of the Hall. In 1699 the music-room was repaired; in 1707 a lion and unicorn was put up in the court-room.

The third, and present, Ironmongers' Hall was erected from the designs of T. Holden, and at a cost of about 5,000*l.*, about 1748. It was not completed until 1750, when, on February 13 that year, a ball was given at the opening, and a hogshead of port wine, half a chest of oranges, and other good things were consumed at the feast. A full description of the Hall and its interesting contents will be found in Malcolm's "Londinium Redivivum," vol. ii. 1803, pp. 32-62. The Hall was repaired in 1817, and in 1827 a light corridor connecting the grand staircase with the drawing-room was erected, and two years later the four handsome columns and pilasters were put up in the drawing-room. Just about a century after the erection of the present Hall it underwent an entire redecoration, and was reopened once more with a ball on June 8, 1847. The banqueting-room is 70 feet long and 29 feet wide. A carved panelled dado, 8 feet high, is carried round the room, having in the upper compartments the arms in proper colours of the past masters from the recognised foundation in 1351. The windows, as seen from the street, are curious as presenting seven different styles, and only equalled, we believe, by a house in Berkeley Square, where, out of eleven windows, seven are of different kinds. Mr. Nicholl gives a full description of the Hall and its contents as existing in 1866 in his "Some Account," pp. 421–467. The portraits of eminent members hang on the walls of the banqueting-room and in the court-room, two of the latest in the latter room being those of Mr. John Nicholl, F.S.A., the Company's historian, and Mr. S. Adams Beck, who for nearly fifty years was the clerk and sincere friend of the Company, as mentioned in our last chapter.

From Ironmongers' Hall were conducted the last remains of many a notable member or citizen in the olden time. The funeral pall or hearse cloth used on these occasions was the gift of John Gyva, ironmonger, in 1515, and Elizabeth, his wife. It is of crimson velvet and cloth of gold tissue, and is described and illustrated at pages 454-7 of Mr. French's "Catalogue." Notes of the sixteenth century funerals are given in "The Diary of Henry Machyn" (Camden Society), 1848. In the "Diary of Samuel Pepys" he tells us of the funeral from the Hall in November, 1662, of Sir Richard Stayner, where "good rings" were distributed and the mourners had "a four-horse coach," in which he by mistake took a place.

There have been many meetings at the Hall, some of national and others of great civic interest, especially in the making free and entertainments to distinguished men like Lords Hood and Exmouth. In 1694 the Company let the Hall for a lottery, which was called "the best and fairest chance at last," and five years later the whole of the old armour then standing in and about the premises was sold to Mr. Thomas Saunders for eight guineas, "the musketts 2*s*. 6*d*. apiece!" It is not generally known that the national anthem of "God Save the King," so repeatedly sung at the old City feasts and all over the world, was the composition of Dr. John Bull, who, with the children of the King's Chapel, sung and played it before James I. and Prince Henry at the Merchant Taylors' Hall feast, July 16, 1607. In Ironmongers' Hall have dined Dr. Livingstone, Admiral Dawes, and Sir Garnet Wolseley, the latter just before leaving England for the Gold Coast. An interesting article, entitled "Banqueting with the Ironmongers," and giving a good picture of these modern entertainments, appeared in the *City Press*, August 21, 1875. The Company's plate is not so extensive as that possessed by some of the City Guilds. The collection will be found described by Mr. French in his "Catalogue," pp. 616-624. There are two mazer bowls (thirteenth to sixteenth century drinking-vessels), of which only fifty are supposed to be extant, and therefore curious and interesting. They are described by Mr. St. John Hope in "Archæologia," vol. 50, 1887, pp. 129-193. In the old views of the exterior of the Hall are shown the houses on the east side adjoining Billiter Street. These were pulled down and rebuilt some twenty years ago. Finally, in bringing our description of the Hall to a close, we cannot forbear mentioning a curious fact. In the first report of the City Livery Companies' Commission, 1884, p. 36, there is a list given of all the existing halls of the City Guilds, thirty-four in number, and yet the Ironmongers' (one of the twelve) has been omitted!

We shall conclude this chapter by noticing the Irish estate of the Ironmongers' Company, called "The Manor of Lizard," about seven miles from Coleraine, and skirting the river Bann, in the province of Ulster, the total area of which is between 12,000 and 13,000 acres, occupied as 550 holdings, with a population of about 2,800 persons all told. The net receipts from rents come to about 4,000*l.* a year. The estate is scattered over five parishes, and until recent years has been a great anxiety to the Company, who, having, like other Guilds, in former times let their lands as a whole to certain responsible persons, receiving a yearly rent, found out too late then that these persons, some of whom were resident, grossly neglected the well-being of both the property and the people. In 1766 the Company leased the estate to Josias du Pre, Esq., for sixty-one years and three lives. In 1813 he sold the remainder of his lease to the Beresford family. The last life mentioned in the lease was that of the Bishop of Meath, who died in his eighty-third year in 1840. The Hon. the Irish Society reported that year:—"The present holders seem only to have used the property for the purpose of making the most of it during the term of their lease," consequently when the Company took possession they found it no easy matter to put the estate in that order which they so long desired to do. Through their energetic agents they have at last succeeded, after terribly uphill work, and we believe the tenantry now find out the truth of the Irish Society's report in 1838, which stated, "This estate upon the death of the Bishop of Meath passes into the hands of the Company, and we have no doubt that it will prove a source of much happiness to the tenantry when they shall be placed under the immediate superintendence of that body."

The origin of the purchase of this estate arose through the rebellion in Ireland, in the reign of Elizabeth, when the O'Neills and the O'Dohertys were in the possession of the province of Ulster. In order to suppress the revolt the army was sent over in 1566, and encamped in Derry County. The lands were subsequently confiscated, and when James I. came to the throne he found them such a source of trouble that he or his Ministers devised the scheme of selling the whole property, being, as we have said, confiscated from traitors to the Crown. The King also instituted the order of Baronets to such persons who would pay towards the charges of the reclamation of the waste lands and the new plantation, and peopling with Protestants the North of Ireland, and that is why the red hand of Ulster will be found in a baronet's coat of arms. After much trouble the City of London were offered the Irish estates, which the Companies jointly purchased for 40,000*l.* This sum was subscribed by fifty-five of the Guilds, being the twelve great and forty-three minor Companies. The great ones were to manage for the lesser, the Ironmongers being associated with the Brewers, Scriveners, Coopers, Pewterers, Barbers, Surgeons, and Carpenters, paying 3,333*l.* 6*s.* 8*d.* as their share, calling their portion the Manor of Lizard, from the crest of their arms. "This manor was created by the Irish Society in October, 1618, and was conveyed to the Ironmongers' on November 7 following, to the only use and behoof of the said Company, their successors, and assigns for ever." In May, 1613, the Coopers' Company's share was taken over by the Corporation of London, and the Irish Society of the City of London, incorporated by royal charter March 29, 1613, was made a body corporate to carry out the plantation of the City and County of Londonderry, which cost them from first to last before completed nearly 100,000*l.*

To this day the citizens of London annually visit Ireland, the last visit in 1888 being more than usually important, as the two-hundredth anniversary of the memorable siege of Derry, now Londonderry, in 1688, about which so much has been written and said. The following works may be consulted as giving true details of the plantation scheme, one of, if not the wisest of, the schemes of the first King James :—

"A Concise View of the Irish Society," 1822.

"An Historical Narrative of the Irish Society," 1865.

"An Historical Account of the Plantation in Ulster," by the Rev. Geo Hill, 1877.

"Calendar of the Carew Manuscripts at Lambeth Palace," 1873.

"Derriana : a History of the Siege, &c." by the Rev. John Graham, 1823.

"A True Account of the Siege, &c." by the Rev. George Walker, 1689.

Had it not been for this George Walker and the heroic prentice lads of Derry, the preservation of that city would never have been secured. (See Lord Macaulay's History)

THE HEARSE-CLOTH, OR IRONMONGERS' FUNERAL PALL. 1515.

PLATE III.

The Monstrance or Shrine at each end.

(See page 55.)

CHAPTER VIII.

THE IRONMONGERS' CHARITIES AND CHARITABLE IRONMONGERS.

CITIZENSHIP is the birthright of every man, but it is not every man who is worthy of the name of citizen. What makes the honourable distinction all the more valuable is when "a citizen of no mean city," and the true representative of "a nation of shopkeepers," so truly values his rights and privileges as to be ever ready to come forward when occasion requires to protect it from the ignorance and contamination of those whose only design must be to overthrow its virtues for the sake of personal gains. It was Lord Chancellor Selborne who some years ago publicly declared that his ancestors for four generations had been connected with one of the City Guilds, and he had never been ashamed of anything either of those ancestors had done, and never regretted his own connection with the City or its Companies. And another eminent man of earlier days most emphatically declared, "I would rather be born of the basest and meanest of mankind, and rise to fame and distinction by my own exertions, than that, being born of noble ancestry and high degree, I should bring disgrace on an exalted name, and cross with a bar sinister the proud escutcheon of my father's house."

To the humble traders of old London their richer brethren left their trusts, their charities, and their blessings. Their estates had been obtained by hard work and hard-earned money in a great many instances, and having been associated with the zealous and careful men of their own Guilds they left to them the carrying out of the designs expressed in their wills. No one would have left to a Government department such a trust then, and no one will do so now.

The Government inspector, in his evidence before the Companies Commission, declared that he considered William Thwaytes' bequest of 20,000*l.* "to make the Society comfortable"—and that Society was the Clothworkers' Company, to which he belonged some half a century ago—really meant "to make the traders comfortable"! Or that every clothworker in the kingdom—shall we say the world?—ought to participate. On the same principle, if a workman in a shop left "to the workmen in the shop" 5*l.*, every shop in that trade should have its share. Pray what would be the value of the bequest?

The City Companies, as we have shown in the history of the Ironmongers, had a terribly uphill battle to fight with early monarchy. Whenever there was a chance to rob the citizens, down pounced the Government or Royalty. Henry VIII. commenced by dissolving the religious houses, and the good King Edward VI. seized the properties left to the Companies by the wills of benefactors on the plea that they were for superstitious uses. Having taken possession he was glad enough to sell the property back to them, so that he made a very profitable business of the transaction. The result of this "clever" and "sharp" practice was that the Ironmongers had to sell their private property to buy back the trust estate. Having done this, is it not creditable to a City Company to be still administering that trust of which the King himself had originally deprived them?

Coming down to more modern times, Thomas Betton, Hoxton Square, Shoreditch, left the Ironmongers' Company, in 1723, the residue of his estate for the purpose of redeeming slaves in Barbary. Other notable citizens had done a similar good deed before then, for so long previous as 1641 Roger Abdy, merchant, had left 120*l.* "for or towards the ransoming and redeeming of sixe poore English Protestant captives out of the bondage and slavery of the Turks." Thomas Betton's bequest was a noble one, for just about the date of it all the world was suffering from the terrors of slavery. Between 1734 and 1825 the Company appears to have paid away in redemption money something like 21,000*l.*, or as much as the whole estate had been originally worth but the Ironmongers, having been good trustees, had "improved" the estate, and the result was that after Lord Exmouth's great victory, no more slaves being likely to be redeemable, and there being a large balance at the bank, the Company desired to utilise the surplus for the benefit of charity, reserving a certain sum per annum for future redemptions and contingencies. This was serious, so down came the Government and popped the whole into Chancery. The Company believed they were right, and did not want the interference; but they had to fight against the Crown, and from 1829 to 1845 did the battle last. Several thousands of pounds did Government law cost the charity, but that the Company was right is evident, because the highest tribunal, the House of Lords, decided that what the Company had proposed so many years before should now be carried out—bequests to the poor of the company and to every national school in the kingdom.

The Ironmongers' charities are not so extensive as many of the other City Guilds', but they represent a variety of really good and seasonable benefactions. Among these are two almshouse foundations (Geffery and Lewen), scholarships to schools and exhibitions to universities, a small free school in Cornwall, the poor of the City wards, loans to poor young freemen to help them on in life, bequests to hospitals, to poor maids upon their marriage, to poor prisoners in debt, to the poor freemen and their widows, to poor ministers and clergy, to the national schools of the kingdom, &c. The charity trusts amount to about 12,000*l.* a year, half of which, being from rents, have of late years fluctuated. The Company does not possess any ecclesiastical patronage, except the appointment of a chaplain, who is also the minister to the almshouse poor. There was a priest of the company 400 years ago, but the present chaplain, the Rev. H. M. Baker, is the fourteenth since 1715, when the first appointment to the almshouses in the Kingsland Road was made.

Through the changes of the times and the "compulsory" sales by Act of Parliament for modern improvements, some of the old property has changed hands and new property has been purchased. This has been specially the case under the Geffery and Betton trusts, and round about East and West Ham and the Isle of Dogs. The Company now possesses houses and premises in Old Street, St. Luke's (Mitchell),

Basinghall Street, Philpot Lane, and Fleet Street. It also possesses the site of the famous New Park Street Chapel, Southwark, where the Rev. C. H. Spurgeon first preached when he came to London; also, farms in the counties of Bucks, Essex, and Surrey. When in the good old times—so says a newspaper in July, 1769—the Company went on tour to view their Essex estate, they "held their annual feast at the Devil's House" (now Duval's House), near East Ham, a house of entertainment at that date. The sign of the house is suggestive to the disciples of St. Dunstan. In recent years two great districts have grown up in and around East and West Ham—Beckton, which takes its name from the worthy clerk of the Company (S. Adams Beck), who died in 1883, and Silvertown, from a recent Master of the Ironmongers' Company (S. W. Silver), who has proved most energetic in promoting the Company's welfare. One word more about the old estates. The great fire of London of 1666 burnt down nearly all the City property of the Companies, and the loss to the Ironmongers was serious. Fortunately, the Hall was saved.

Charitable Ironmongers, whether we view them as donors of land, of houses, of plate, or other things, or for the time they have given towards promoting the welfare of the Company, have been in many ways worthy benefactors to the City and the citizens. We have been curious in one inquiry—to what extent the donations of some classes of plate have been made, and we find that in the 400 years ending 1865 "brother" Ironmongers have given twenty-nine silver gilt cups and covers, many very large and valuable, seventeen basins and ewers, and seven salts; besides many other descriptions of plate, such as silver spoons, ornaments, candlesticks, and the like. Of course, the Company does not possess all the valuables now. Our former Monarchy, who had the citizens' welfare so much at heart, took good care (as we have already shown) not to allow these valuables to remain too long in the hands of "the City Fathers," and so to-day the Ironmongers have but a small collection of plate. When the charitable Ironmongers left these cups for their brethren "to make themselves comfortable," whether at a dinner or other feast, they never thought that their radically-inclined descendants would object to the good old English greeting: "The Master and Wardens drink to you in a loving cup, and bid you all a hearty welcome."

Eminent Ironmongers, by their portraits, still adorn the Ironmongers' Hall. Thirteen are in the banqueting-room, and eight in the court-room. Armorial shields round the Hall give us the names of our worthy Masters from the earliest times, while there are two statues of great interest, Edward IV., the founder, and Lord Mayor Beckford—this latter being in a niche on the grand staircase.

Abstracts of most of the Ironmongers' wills are in our collection, and the series is most curious. We cannot do justice to the subject now, but some time we hope to give some interesting details. One, however, is worth quoting, and that is of Alderman Richard Chamberlin, 1567. He was a good benefactor, he remembered the poor, he gave the Company 50*l.* "to helpe them oute of debte," he left 10*l.* for "a dynner at oure halle," desiring the members' wives should be present, and he then put down on paper, "I praye God make us merye in Heaven!"

We will now, in alphabetical arrangement, give a few of the names of those Ironmongers worth remembering. We do not profess to give a complete list, for such would form a volume by itself, so numerous are they, and so many notes do we possess about them.

BATE, John, 1500, and Felys his wife, gave to the Company a cup and other things, "ther with to do God and us worship, and not to be solde while they will last."

BECKFORD, William, Alderman, and Lord Mayor 1762 and 1770, when he died; was made free of the Company 1752 was born in Jamaica, his father being Peter Beckford, Speaker in the Assembly. The Lord Mayor made himself famous by his celebrated speech to George III., as engraved on the monument in Guildhall. Another statue, formerly at Fonthill, was presented to the company by his son William in 1833. See pedigrees and other details in Britton and Rutter's two descriptions of Fonthill, Wilts. Richard, brother of the Lord Mayor, was also Alderman and M.P., but he was a member of the Clothworkers' Company.

BETTON, Thomas, a Turkey merchant, admitted to the freedom by redemption 1696, lived in Hoxton Square; will dated 1723. He died 1724; buried in the Ironmongers' Almshouse Grounds, Kingsland Road. Portrait presented to the Company in 1728. Gave the residue of his estate for the redemption of slaves in Barbary (as already noted).

BLUNDELL, Peter, although not an Ironmonger, but from a poor errand boy had grown to be a rich clothier, and one of "the worthies of Devon" (Prince), and "a man very Godly and Christianly disposed all his life time" (Stow), left charities to the extent of about 40,000*l.*, including 150*l.* to each of the twelve great Livery Companies of London. He died 1601, aged eighty-one.

BICKNELL, Elhanan, of Herne Hill, Dulwich, a citizen and Ironmonger, and great patron of the arts. He died 1861. His will was proved at 350,000*l.* His pictures sold at Christie's for 56,499*l.*; the sculpture, 2,145*l.*; drawings, 15,947*l.*; prints, 444*l.*; his houses and lands, 18,000*l.* He had no fewer than ten Turner's in his collection. He left several charitable bequests.

CAMBELL.—Several of this family have proved to be eminent Ironmongers. Sir Thomas, Lord Mayor 1610, Master 1604 and 1613; Sir James, Lord Mayor 1629, and three times Master; Robert, a merchant, and Master 1631. Sir James was the principal benefactor, leaving nearly 50,000*l.*, as may be seen in Strype's "Stow." He died 1641, and his portrait is in the Hall.

CANNING.—Of this family William was Master 1617 and 1627, when he died. George (who died 1646) was for many years the Company's agent in Ireland, and was the ancestor of the Prime Minister George Canning.

CARRE, John, 1571, his son in 1573, and Mrs. Carre in 1583, left many bequests to the Company.

CHAMBERLIN.—This family was well represented on the Company. There were Richard, George, and Robert. Alderman Richard, Master 1560 and 1565, died November 19, 1566, and was buried in St. Olave, Old Jewry. His epitaph stated:—

To the poore he was liberall and gave for God's sake,
But now his fame is plentifull and he a Heavenly make;
He was like one of vs, according to our mould,
But now he unlike vs in Heaven where he would;
His time was short in sicknesse rare as to all is knowne,
But now his time shall long endure and never be cast downe.

CLITHEROW.—Alderman and Lord Mayor Sir Christopher; Master 1618-1624; died 1642. He was son of Henry, three times Master, who died 1607. See pedigree in the "History of Hertfordshire." A worthy benefactor.

DANE, William, Alderman and Sheriff 1569, Master 1570-1573; died November, 1579. Margaret, his widow, 1579, was "a good woman." She left many charities, including the 12,000 faggots to the poor for firewood, which has been made by the ignorant the more serious gift to burn them with. Her portrait hangs in the Hall.

DENHAM, Sir William, descended from the Dinhams of Normandy. Sheriff 1534, Master 1531 to 1548. Died August 4, 1548. By a curious error in the codicil to the will the Company were compelled to purchase the properties previously bequeathed to them, including that known as the Old Jewry Chambers. His portrait hangs in the Hall. Curiously enough, a branch of the Denham family were copyholders of Hackney in the reign of James I., and removed to Plumstead. Of later years another branch resided in Hackney, and the wife of the present writer is a descendant of that branch, descended from the Alderman Denham, and from the Thomas Denham, a City Corporator early this century, and a member of the Court of the Ironmongers' Company.

DOWNE, Robert, in 1556, gave premises in St. Sepulchre; also for dinners, obits and plate. The site "Ironmongers' Buildings" is now covered by the Holborn Valley Viaduct.

DRAPER, Sir Christopher, Lord Mayor, 1566. Eight times Master, the last time in 1581. A window formerly existing at the Hall, with his portrait on it, was removed in 1845.

EAST, Robert, 1606, gave tapestry to the Hall, and 10*l.* for "a drinckinge" at his burial.

FRENCH, George Russell, son of John French, Master 1823. The son was chosen surveyor to the Company May, 1849. He was a Shakespearean antiquary, and wrote many interesting works, especially the compilation "Catalogue of Antiquities" we have so often alluded to. He compiled a very curious list of the Ironmongers' Company, applying to each a Shakespearean quotation. He died in October, 1881.

GEFFERY, Sir Robert, Lord Mayor 1686, Master 1667 and 1685. He died 1703, and was buried in St. Dionis, Fenchurch Street, and when that church was pulled down his remains were removed, July, 1878, to the Ironmongers' burial-ground, Kingsland Road. By will, after many charitable bequests, he left the residue of his estate for the purchase of land, and the erection (in 1714) of the present chapel and fourteen almshouses. The old twenty-nine rules for the government will be found in Strype's "Stow." At the date of their erection the almshouses were in "the suburbs."

GRINSELL, Thomas, "Citizen and Ironmonger," a well-known parishioner of St. Dunstan's-in-the-West, Fleet Street, and famous for having been the Master of "the gentle angler, Izaak Walton, who became a member of the Company in 1618. The Grinsell family subsequently resided in Westminster. About Thomas, see "Memorials of Temple Bar and Fleet Street," 1869, p. 80.

GYVA, John, about 1515 gave to the Company the hearse-cloth or funeral-pall. It is of crimson velvet and cloth-of-gold tissue, ornamented with fruit and flowers for centre-piece. In the centre of each sides the Blessed Virgin Mary in glory crowned as Queen of Heaven, with figures of Saint Elizabeth of Hungary, St. John Baptist, and St. John Evangelist. Beyond the figures on each side the Company's arms, and at each end in cloth of gold a monstrance, representing a silver-gilt shrine, jewelled, inscribed with the name and date of John Gyva and Elizabeth, his wife. This pall was long used for funerals. In 1532 it was only to be used by members and their wives, but this exception was relaxed, for in 1678 40*s*. was to be the fee for its use by strangers generally. Elizabeth Gyva in 1534 gave the Company a tenement, directing them to "remember" her in their prayers for 100 years.

HALLWOOD, Thomas, 1622, gave plate, exhibitions to universities, &c. His portrait hangs in the Hall.

HANBEY, Thomas, 1782, provided for the education of two children in Christ's Hospital, and Mary, his wife, 1796, left the interest of 300*l*. to provide for the repairs of the tomb of her husband in St. Luke's Churchyard, Old Street, and residue of the interest among the poor.

HANDSON, Ralph, clerk to the Company, was a good benefactor and kindly disposed, leaving in 1653 to the poor members, to hospitals, and to the yeomanry for their half-yearly repast, as already mentioned. His portrait hangs in the Hall. He was cousin to Nicholas Leat.

HEYLIN, Rowland, Sheriff 1624, Master 1614 and 1625, died 1629. He gave 300*l*., out of which a dinner and a sermon were to be annually provided to commemorate the Powder Plot deliverance, and loans made to poor young freemen. His portrait is in the Hall.

HARVEY, Sir James, Alderman; Lord Mayor 1582; four times Master. His son, Sir Sebastian, was Lord Mayor 1618, Master 1600; wrote his name "Harvye." Lady Harvey, 1620, gave 21*l*. for a dinner at the funeral of Sir Sebastian.

HOOD, Samuel, first Viscount, was presented with the freedom 1783 in honour of his great victory. He died 1816. His portrait by Gainsborough (presented by Lord Hood) hangs in the Hall. We possess a characteristic letter written by Lord Hood in 1811 with his left hand.

HUMFREYS, Sir William, Bart., Lord Mayor 1714, Master 1705, and gave a silver cup and cover. He acted as chief butler at the coronation of George I. Died 1735, buried at St. Mildred's, Poultry, and when that church was pulled down (1875) the Company desired to give him a "proper" reinterment at Ilford, but, although the character of the coffin showed that the body inside was possibly his, all the silver plates and handles and ornaments had been stolen long before, and so Sir William could not be identified, and the remains were taken with the others.

LANE, Ralph, Turkey merchant, gave to the Company, in 1712, a silver-gilt cup, upon which is engraved a coat of arms, with thirty-two quarterings. It is interesting to note that John Lane, the elder, in 1457, was one of the Company who advanced 10*l*. towards purchasing the Hall property. His son John gave 40*s*.

LAWRENCE.—A well-known and respected name in the City. Several have been members of the Company. John Lawrans, about 1500, gave "a grete maser which hath sent Lawrans in the bottom." It weighed over 60 oz. Another

John Lawrence, in 1731, gave a tankard. We may here mention that

ST. LAWRENCE is the patron saint of the company. The old barge "head" represented the saint with the gridiron in his hand. In the early churchwarden's accounts of the parish of St. Lawrence, Reading, are numerous curious entries between 1520 and 1530, such as:—"For gildyng of Seynt Lawrence gredyron, viij*d*."; "to the peynters Wyff, dew for gilding of Seynt Lawren, vj*s*. viij*d*.," &c.

LEAT, Nicholas, Alderman, three times Master, died 1631, captain of the trained bands. He was an authority in agriculture (*see* Gerard's "Herbal," 1597, p. 246). The sons presented his portrait now in the court-room.

LEWEN, Thomas, Alderman and Sheriff, Master 1535, died 1557, founded the almshouses in Bread Street, now in St. Luke's. A good benefactor. His portrait is in the Hall.

MITCHELL, Thomas, died 1527, gave "a croft of garden enclosed by ditches and wall" outside Cripplegate (now St. Luke's) of about 10 acres, which, with about an acre purchased in 1595, comprises now 11½ acres, covered with some 360 houses. St. Luke's Church was built and churchyard formed on part of the ground. Portrait in Hall.

MORRIS, Richard, was Master in the Armada year, 1588. Many members of the family have been in the Company between 1568 and 1718. He died 1592. His daughter married first Sir William Cockayne (Lord Mayor, 1619), and, secondly, Henry Carey, Earl of Dover. From both husbands peerages descend. Samuel Morris, in 1680, gave an iron box, with keys, to hold the Company's seal.

MILNE, Sir David, K.C.B., admitted to the Freedom of the Company with his superior officer, Lord Exmouth, in 1817.

NEWELL, Mrs. Ann, in 1544, gave a table and napkins —a seasonable gift in those days. Her namesake, William J. Newall, who died a liveryman of the Company in 1888, and worth 257,000*l*., seems to have forgotten in his will his poor "brother-ironmongers"!

NICHOLL.—This is an old family name on the company John Nicholl, of Canonbury, Master 1859, was a good friend to the Company (and to the writer). He compiled a magnificent account of the history of the Ironmongers, 1851 and 1866, and the original MS. "Records," in six volumes, are in the Company's library. He died February 7, 1871, aged eighty-one, and his portrait appropriately hangs in the court-room next to that of Mr. Beck. His son, Edward Hadham Nicholl, Esq., is the senior warden of the Company this year.

PELLATT.—Many representatives of this Sussex family have been in the Company, including Apsley Pellatt, M.P., died 1863 (who gave a silver-mounted snuff-box), and Thomas Pellatt, Clerk of the Company, died 1829. Apsley Pellatt, of Lewes, grandfather of the M.P., was Master 1789.

PELLEW, Edward, created Viscount Exmouth, 1816. The hero of Algiers and the terminator of slavery there. Presented with the freedom of the Company, January 31, 1817, and with a sword by the City. The original grant of the Company's freedom, signed by T. Pellatt, the clerk, is in the possession of a member of the Company. Portrait by Sir William Beechey hangs in the Hall.

PRICE.—This family has had many representatives in the Company. John Price was buried at Clapham 1739; his wife 1760. Sir Charles Price, Bart., Lord Mayor 1803, was Master 1798. In his mayoralty he gave the magnificent cut-glass chandelier now hanging in the Hall. His portrait also hangs there. Among other papers the writer has the original Privy Seal for the grant of the baronetcy. Sir Charles died 1818. His son was Master 1819 and died 1847. He was succeeded by Sir Charles Rugge Price, who had a splendid collection of engravings, including a choice copy of Rembrandt's "Hundred Guilder Piece"—Christ Healing the Sick—which at the sale in 1867 sold for 1,180*l.*, the highest sum ever paid for a single engraving.

SHAKESPEARE, John, Alderman and Sheriff 1768, translated to the Ironmongers' from the Broderers' 1767, Master 1769. A large ropemaker at Shadwell. Buried at Stepney, 1775. Gave silver candlesticks to the Company. He was supposed to be descended from a branch of the dramatist's family.

SLADE, Felix, son of Robert, of Doctors' Commons, and Walcot Place, Lambeth; Master 1803. The son was a collector of choice articles and a great benefactor to the British Museum and the nation. He died March 29, 1868. He founded the Slade Professorship.

THOMPSON, William, Alderman, M.P. Lord Mayor 1828 A wealthy ironfounder. Master 1829 and 1841; died 1854 His only daughter married the Earl of Bective, now Marquis of Headfort. Among his gifts were two large silver candlesticks.

THOROLD.—Several members have been on the Company and served offices of Master, &c.; also benefactors to the poor. The family were of Harmeston Hall, county Lincoln, which was sold in 1884 for 115,000*l.*

WALKER, Henry, made free in 1634, having served apprentice to Robert Holland, was so extraordinary an individual that John Taylor wrote and printed his "Life and Progress of Henry Walker the Ironmonger," 1642, and it is now a very rare tract. Captain William Walker, Master 1684, gave in 1694 a large set of knives and forks, with silver handles, for the Company's future use.

WALTON, Izaak, "the gentle angler," apprentice to Thomas Grinsell, was, on November 18, 1618, "admitted and sworne a free brother of this companie and payd for his admittance xiij*d.* and for default of presentment and enrollment xs.'. His portrait hangs in the Hall. He was warden of the Yeomanry 1627, died December 15, 1683, and buried at Winchester. A full account of him and his family will be found in the "Memorials of Temple Bar and Fleet Street," 1869, p. 82, and Pink's and Wood's "Clerkenwell," p. 107. The writer possesses a large amount of curious and original matter relating to "good Izaak," which he intends one day to publish.

WESTWOOD.—Several have been members. While Robert was Master, 1828, among the eighty-five liverymen were Lord Exmouth, Sir David Milne, two baronets, and two aldermen. Robert, Master in 1861, gave a silver-gilt cup and cover. William Henry, in 1878 and 1882, proved himself very kindly disposed to the Company's poor.

WOODWARD, Mistress Katherine, in the seventeenth century, left 200*l*. for poor scholars, prisoners, hospitals, and poor maids' marriages.

YOUNG, Richard, 1675, gave a silver salt, a caudle cup and cover, and was excused serving office of Master. John, in 1695, gave the Company six pictures.

Such, then, are a few of the names of Ironmongers worthy to be remembered. We have not exhausted, by a very long way, our list, but we think the selection will prove that the Ironmongers have had many good and true citizens in their roll. Our wish is this: May they increase as years roll on, and, as the toast is periodically given by the Master of the Company, so do we echo it three times three — "The Worshipful Company of Ironmongers, Root and Branch, and may it Flourish for Ever!"

The writer having so far completed the task he has set himself, and briefly chronicled some of the most interesting facts connected with his ancient Company, thinks it but right to say that what he has now printed is only a small portion of a larger history, which some time hence he intends to produce for the benefit of the public at large, if his life is spared to undertake the work. Having been honoured by his brother freemen, as already stated in the last chapter, he determined to prove he was not unmindful of his duty, or the rights and privileges of his brethren, whatever some persons may think to the contrary. He has, therefore, ventured to print as succinct an account of their history as it is possible to give in a small compass, and Herbert's "History," and the "Some Account" of his old friend John Nicholl being either out of print or too expensive, probably the present will do as a temporary substitute for the members until another is ready for publication.

T. C. NOBLE,

Warden of the Yeomanry,
1888–1889.

THE DEVIL GIVES ST. DUNSTAN A MORNING CALL.

ST. DUNSTAN COMPELS THE "EVIL ONE" TO SIGN A TREATY OF PEACE

APPENDIX.

THE BLACKSMITHS' COMPANY.

THE advance of technical education, the inauguration of another trades exhibition promoted by a City Company, and that Company the ancient Blacksmiths' Guild, must be our excuse for placing upon record some account of its history from the earliest date known about it as a fraternity.

Of the origin of Guilds we have already had occasion to speak in our history of the Ironmongers. Mr. Nicholl, the historian of that Company, gives us some interesting facts in his notes, and we cannot do better than quote his preliminary words:—

The art of working in metals was more highly esteemed than any other by the Anglo-Saxons. Their best artisans were the clergy. Edgar established a law that every priest, to increase knowledge, should diligently learn some handicraft. Dunstan, Archbishop of Canterbury, to the arts of music, engraving, painting, and writing, added the craft of a smith, and was an expert workman. Stigand and Ethelwold, both bishops, were celebrated for their mechanical skill. The chief smith was a man of considerable distinction in the courts of the Anglo-Saxon kings and his privileges and weregild exceeded those of any other craftsman. Towards the period of the Conquest the manufacture of iron had considerably increased, and the art of working it was better understood. Steel and iron armour were common. At the time of the Domesday Survey the City of Hereford had six smiths, who paid each one penny for his forge, and made 120 pieces of iron from the king's ore, receiving in return a customary payment of three pence, and being free from all other service. The City of Gloucester paid to the king 36 dicras of iron and 100 ductile rods to make nails for the king's ships. Iron had now become the principal manufacture of Gloucestershire, and in the reign of Edward I. there is stated to have been no less than 72 furnaces in the Forest of Dean for smelting it. The largest establishments of the Romans for the manufacture of iron in Britain were in this county, but the method, whatever it may have been, which they employed was imperfect and the cinders of their numerous forges, wherever they are discovered, are found to contain a very considerable portion of unsmelted metal. The first smelting-furnace, and that which in all probability was used by the Romans for the manufacture of iron, is supposed to be the air-bloomery; it is described as a low conical structure, with small openings at the bottom for the admission of air and a large orifice at top for carrying off the gaseous products of combustion. It was filled with charcoal and ore in alternate layers, and the fire applied to the lowest part. How long this simple contrivance continued in use we have no means of ascertaining, the period to which it belongs being so very remote; there is no doubt, however, that the next era of improvement in the manufacture of iron was the introduction of bellows, and the construction of the blast-bloomery, which greatly facilitated the process of smelting, and, by allowing the construction of larger furnaces, considerably increased the manufacture. The blast-bloomery, in process of time and the constant progression of the arts, was superseded by what is denominated the blast-furnace. This last improvement is supposed to have been introduced during the early part of the sixteenth century; for in the seventeenth century the art of casting in metal had arrived at a great degree of perfection, and in the reign of Elizabeth there was a considerable export trade of cast-iron ordnance to the Continent.

As "by hammer and hand all arts do stand," so was the origin of the Blacksmiths' Guild in the nineteenth year of the reign of Edward III., 1325. Like many others it is a fraternity by prescription, subsequently incorporated by Royal Charter. "The Articles of the Blacksmiths," dated the 46th of Edward III., A.D. 1372, are enrolled in Letter-book G, fo. 285, preserved among the Guildhall records, and a most interesting and concise translation will be found in Mr. Riley's "Memorials of London," 1868, p. 361. The Articles specially provide against the introduction into the City of inferior foreign-made work, and the forging of trade-marks was, of course, a serious matter. "Every master in the said trade shall put his own mark upon his work, such as heads of lances, knives and axes, and other large work, that people may know who made them in case default shall be found in the same." Forgers of such mark were dealt with without delay, and it is interesting to know that one of the earliest of the overseers appointed resided near Holborn Bridge (now the Viaduct), close to the Charity Trust Estate of the present Company. No one was to be made free of the Guild unless he was skilled in his work as an apprentice should be, so that we may be sure the early blacksmiths truly represented their "art and mystery."

"The Ordinances of the Blacksmiths" are enrolled in the Guildhall "Letter-book" H., fo. 292, and will be found translated in Mr. Riley's "Memorials," p. 537. They are dated the 18 Richard 2nd, 1394. No smith was to work throughout the night, or to annoy his neighbours, and the hours of work were to be from 6 o'clock in the morning to 8 o'clock in the evening in winter, and from the beginning of daylight to 9 o'clock at night in summer. None to work in his shop on a Saturday, or on the eve of a feast or holy day after the first stroke of the vesper bell, under heavy fines and penalties. Two wardens to be annually elected for their government, and strict search to be made in the City and suburbs for the detection of false wares. No one to make a key for a lock unless he have the lock to make it by, and nothing to be exposed for sale at any fair until the wardens have certified it "good and lawful."

Forty years afterwards we find another enrolment, and among records where such an entry would never be looked for—the Register Book of the Commissary of London, labelled "Liber 3 More, 1418–1438," folio 455, how preserved in the Probate Registry, Somerset House. We are indebted to Mr. J. R. Daniel-Tyssen for the discovery in 1852, and to Mr. H. C. Coote for editing and printing them in the

"Transactions of the London and Middlesex Archæological Society," Vol. IV., pp. 32–35. They are entitled—

Ordynances articulis, and constitucions ordeyned and grarnted by the Worshypfull Maistres and Wardeynes in the Worship of the Bretherhed of Saynt Loye, att the Fest of Ester, with alle the hole company of the crafte of blaksmythes, who assemble in Seynt Thomas of Acres and thence to the Grey Freres of London. Founded and ordeyned atte the Fest of Ester, 1434, 12 Henry VI.

These ordinances provide—that every servant (brother) pay 2*d*. quarterly, and every sister 1*d*. Strangers "for yncomyng," pay 2*s*. A beadle of the Yeomanry to be appointed who was to receive from every brother "for his salari" one-halfpenny quarterly. "And whaune eny brother other sisster be passed to God the seyd bedell to have for his traveyle ij*d*." Any member disobeying the orders "to be corrected be the Oversseer," and disobeying the second time he "schalbe put oute of the crafte for evere." New masters were to be chosen at the feast of St. Loy. "If therbe eny brother that telleth the Counseyle of the seyd Bretbered to his master prentis or to eny other man he shall paye to the box ij*s*." Any brother scandalising another to be fined 12*d*. "Also at the quarter dai we will have baken conys as hit was be gonne." Any master breaking the rule to pay 6*s*. 8*d*. All fines were halved—a moiety each to "the Mastres box," and the Yeomen's box. After some other orders follow a list of the fellowship members, sixty-seven in number, headed by John Lamborn, who was then, or had been, "Master of the Yomen." Two of those signing the rules were the wives of two of the brethren, Stephen Manne and William Mapull.

Although the Blacksmiths' Guild was not in existence when St. Dunstan played his harp, and worked at his forge and anvil, we cannot forbear saying something about a prelate who has, more than any other, raised the reputation of the "art and mystery," which after 500 years still flourishes within the boundaries of great London City, and at the time we are writing this gives a splendid proof that it is not wanting in will or way to attempt the improvement of the trade by advocating and supporting technical education.

Dunstan, to whose memory so many churches have been dedicated, was born near Glastonbury, in county Somerset, and educated at the Abbey. In subsequent years, when he passed a retired life, he built himself a small cell, and enacted there (if tradition holds its own) one of, if not the greatest miracle upon record. He was a favourite with King Athelstan, whom he much pleased by musical performances on his harp, and many astounding tales have been handed down to us about this instrument playing without being touched, and rendering such musical and hitherto unknown melody as enabled the humbler classes to be much imposed upon. Dunstan died May 18, A.D. 988, so that he has been dead just 900 years. And yet to-day is still recorded that marvellous meeting he once had with "the evil one," or, as we were told in our youth, the Devil. Many a time did this tempter "try his hand" upon our musical blacksmith. He appeared to him in every shape and form, even as a beautiful female, and certainly to our mind the most likely "to draw." Poor Dunstan in his little cell at Glastonbury, whenever at his devotional practice as harpist, or using his forge and anvil as blacksmith, was certain to receive a visit, and his sweet song drowned by the black visitor's unholy jeers. At last the day of reckoning came, Dunstan seized a golden opportunity when his tyrannical tormenter put in appearance at the very time his forge was at work and his pincers hot. Little was said, no doubt, but the doings were great—the greatest ever recorded of man's work—for

> St. Dunstan, so the story goes,
> Seized his sable Majesty by the nose,
> And made him loudly roar;
> So loud, indeed, from North to South,
> From East to West, like from thunder's mouth
> It echoed a thousand miles and more.

But the pulling of the evil one's nose was but a part of the transaction, for our blacksmith then and there pulled out his parchment and made the enemy sign that famous declaration, never in future to molest Holy Church or Holy men, and keep aloof of all buildings in which hang the horseshoe. It is not many years ago that in two streets in London this emblem of protection or "luck" may have been seen—Dudley Street, St. Giles's, and Dean Street, Fetter Lane—the latter place not a thousand miles, but only a few yards, from where this account is printed. As for the hammer, anvil and tongs of St. Dunstan, Mr. Lower in his notices of the ironworks of Sussex, gives woodcuts of the three articles, said to be "the famous originals, preserved at Mayfield in that county, so noted for its iron. The anvil and tongs are of no great antiquity, but the hammer with its iron handle may be considered a mediæval relic." A few years ago we attended a sale of curiosities of more than the usual interest, and which were the lifelong attention of Mr. Snoxall, Charterhouse Square. One of the lots was the original anvil and hammer of the "Harmonious Blacksmith," from which Handel composed his celebrated song, and we can endorse, from a trial we made, the assertion of the MS. description that Powell's anvil produced B and E notes, as few anvils have done, or are likely to do again.

St. Dunstan is the patron saint of the Goldsmiths' Company, and he figures in their hall both in picture and in statue. The legend was a favourite one in their Lord Mayor's Show, especially in that of 1687, when in the trade pageant the prelate seated on a chair of State, having a golden mitre on his head, a crozier in one hand and tongs in the other, surrounded by forges and anvils and blacksmith at work, taught the devil the oft-repeated lesson not to intrude on forbidden ground. We might multiply evidences of the popularity of the famous legend, but we have said enough, and must proceed with our Company's history.

In the first year of the reign of Henry VII. (1485) both the Blacksmiths' and Spurriers' guilds will be found in the list given by Campbell, vol. i. p. 4; and a few years later, in 1502, standing in precedency the 36th Company, the Blacksmiths had a livery of sixteen, and the Spurriers, standing the 46th, had six. When Henry VIII. and Queen Katherine "shall pass by towards their Coronation," the same Companies sent members to represent them, and in the eighth year of that King's reign, 1517, it was settled that in precedency in the future the Blacksmiths should be the 41st Company and the Spurriers the 46th. There were then about sixty Companies in the City, but of these ten were not in the "clothing," that is to say, had a livery.

It was by Charter, dated April 20, 1571, that the two Companies were united under the usual conditions of a body corporate and with the powers and privileges of making

ST. DUNSTAN GIVES A PRACTICAL REMINDER OF THE POWER OF THE HORSE-SHOE.

ordinances for the government of the Company. The Charter was confirmed by James I. in his second year, March 21, 1604-5. Meanwhile the precepts poured into the Blacksmiths as they did to other Companies, and in May, 1595, out of 12,000 quarters of corn stored at the Bridgehouse in the preceding November by the City Guilds, only some 779 quarters remained, and ten of these belonged to this Company. The Corn Custom, as described by Herbert, was a heavy tax, and often so tyrannical was the system of levy that some of the wardens were sent to prison in 1632 for neglecting to obey orders.

In 1609 King James I. submitted to the City of London his scheme for the plantation of the forfeited lands of the O'Neills and the O'Dohertys in the province of Ulster in the North of Ireland; and the same King founded a new order of Knighthood, purchasable by those desirous of helping to maintain the authority of the King in future against the rebels in Ireland. That order of Knighthood is the present Baronetage, and in proof of its origin every person so titled bears in his shield of arms the red hand of Ulster. The citizens of London paid James I., from first to last, for their Ulster estates more than 60,000*l.* The difficulty then arose as to the management, and so, in 1613, the whole property was partitioned off into twelve shares (according to the sum subscribed by each of the twelve principal Guilds, who, having raised 40,000*l.*, showed that each of the twelve had paid 3,333*l.* 6*s.* 8*d.*). With the twelve principal companies certain minor ones, having paid a certain sum, joined in the scheme, and accordingly, the Blacksmiths, subscribing 64*l.* with seven others, became associated with the Vintners, who held possession until the year 1736, when they sold the whole estate, reserving only a rent charge.

There are many interesting documents extant relating to the Blacksmiths and the Blacksmiths' Company. We do not lack the will to publish all the information we could give about their progress, but for the greatest of all reasons—want of room, our space being but limited—we must limit our notes to a few of the most important events.

In 1607 Thomas Bickford, Master of the Company, prosecuted Nicholas Lowe for carrying on the trade of a smith, he not being free of the City; and in March, 1612, the curious controversy about Daubigny's patent set all the machinery of the Royal Commissioners and the City into high-pressure activity. It appears that Clement Dawbney, *alias* Daubigny, desired to have a renewal of his patent for cutting iron into small rods, and that restraint should be placed upon the importation of foreign iron so cut. His petition to the Commissioners of Suits was backed by shipwrights, masters, and nailmakers, who particularly condemned foreign iron. The Commissioners, being unable to decide, referred the matter to three of the City Companies, the Ironmongers, Blacksmiths, and Carpenters. The record books of the Ironmongers contain many interesting details of the inquiry made by that company into the question in dispute, and two of the most active members in the debate were two of the Chamberlyn family—George (then Master, in 1612) and Richard (who had been Master two years previous). The Nailmakers reminded the Commissioners, "as the fathers of the Commonwealth," that a private patent deprived the poor of their trade and labour; that one or two enriched themselves at the cost of the many. "Wee allwaies have in evrie C. weight eleven or twelve pounds of ends or refuse iron and pay for that after 2*d.* the lb., whereof we make againe ever hardly a halfpenny for everie pound." Also, "We affirme as workmen that especially it is that the Flemmish iron is as good and servicable and worketh as well as o^{r} owne English iron." The result was a temporary benefit, for the patent was called in; although Sir Francis Bacon, one of the Commissioners, having made a special report subsequently, in 1617, that the monopoly, or patent, would benefit not only the Blacksmiths but the Nailmakers, and was only opposed by Burrell, who had set up a similar ironworks at Danbury, the King renewed the patent, December 11, 1618. The granting of similar monopolies caused no end of bickerings and ill-feeling, and ruin was by no means uncommon among those who neither had capital with which to defend their rights, nor interest at Court to prevent that "bribery and corruption" so common in the surroundings of our seventeenth century monarchy. When, in the previous reign, the Earl of Oxford had endeavoured to obtain one of these patents of privilege against the Company of Pewterers, "whereby he would have undone the pewterers, their wives and families," Queen Elizabeth acted with discretion—not always a virtue with all-powerful royalty—for she actually granted the Earl's desired privilege to the company itself!

We will now give a full copy of a petition which the Blacksmiths sent to the Privy Council in December, 1631. It is directed to "The Right Honble the Lords and others of His Ma^{tys} most Honble Privy Counsell," by "the Mr Wardens and Assistants of the Society of Blacksmiths, London":—

Humbly sheweth—

That notwthstanding yor pet^{rs} great care and good endeav^{r} by making searches and orders, according to their oath and charter, whereby to suppress disorders and abuses in deceitfull working and making of iron-work, yet by the evill example and refractorie of some ill-affected persons of their society, whose names are here under menconed, their authority and orders are slighted and disgraced, and many who have been heretofore obedient and conformable doe now by their meanes continue refractory and disorderly, and yor pet^{rs} and their charters are so notoriously scandalised and abused that of themselves they cannot reforme the same, nor have they any hope of redresse therefore but by yor hono^{rs} favor.

They therefore most humbly beseeche yor hono^{rs} to take their great wrong and just grievance into yor ho^{ble} considerations. And to be pleased to send for the said disorderly and obstinate persons hereunder named before you. And to take such order wth them for their conformity and obedience to the ordinances made and to be made for the good governm^{t} of the said society and prevencon, of deceits & abuses as to y^{r} grave and ho^{ble} wisdome shall seem meete.

And they shall ever praye for yor hono^{rs}.

The names of the six disorderly Blacksmiths appear to have been:—George Johnson, William Bickford, Hanns Garrett, Leonard Berars, William Browne, and Henry Baily. Whether their nonconformity and other troubles led the Company to obtain a new charter we know not, but it is quite clear they did obtain one of Charles I., in his fourteenth year, and dated February 16, 1638-39. By this new grant all persons carrying on the business or trade of a blacksmith or spurrier within the City of London or suburbs four miles round were incorporated as "the Keepers or Wardens and Society of the Art or Mystery of Blacksmiths, London," to have four keepers or wardens and twenty-one assistants, and to make bye-laws and ordinances, to examine all spurs, iron-work made, &c., within the City and four miles round, and to hold lands to the extent of 30*l.* above the former charter allowance of 30*l*. In accordance with this grant and power the Company framed new orders (confirmed by the Judges), dated in December, 1640, and one of these allowed the Company to "call, nominate, choose, and admit into the yeomanry of the said Society such and so many persons being freemen of the said Society as they should think meet, honest, and of ability to be called and admitted into the said yeomanry."

This shows that the Company anciently comprised the Livery, yeomanry, and freemen, and the clerk believes that the freemen were the journeymen and the yeomanry the master blacksmiths. Under the *Quo warranto* writ of Charles II. the Company surrendered with the other Guilds, but were reinstated to their rights and privileges by James II. in the first year of his reign by a charter dated March 18, 1684–85.

The Act of Common Council of June 9, 1658, compelled all persons carrying on the trade to be free of the Company. Fifty years later the Company took special means to enforce it; but, like many of the other rights and privileges of the Guilds, through the altered conditions of trading the power of the Company has not been exercised for many years. The following entry from the books of the Founders' Company, as extracted by Mr. Williams and printed in his "Annals," is sufficiently interesting to merit a place in our present notice of the Blacksmiths:—

1660, Sept. 3. Memorandum.

That upon this day the mast^r and wardens did visit all the founders shopps in Bartholomew Lane and Lothebury—as well of them that were free of the ffounders company as those of the copper-smiths, and found in the shop of John Lucas one lock of brass fitted in wth 20 oz. of lead and one 4-lb. weight unsealed, unsized, and unmarked with the owner's stamp, which work was brought into the Hall.

Founders' Hall stood in Lothbury (hence the name of Founders' Hall Court), and was let to the Electric Telegraph Company in 1853. The Founders of Bartholomew Lane and Lothbury have long since departed to other quarters of the City, and the sites of their ancient trading are now occupied by the great monetary fraternites, the Bank of England and other banks, and the Capel Court of the Stock Exchange.

In May, 1750, the Committee of the Coporation of London specially reported on several petitions presented by masters and journeymen freemen, and it was resolved that the matters complained of required some regulation; that the Court of Aldermen any Tuesday may have the power to grant to any master freeman liberty to employ non-freemen, but under certain restrictions; and that all proceedings and prosecutions rest in the name of the Chamberlain, who, however, only represents the City, and does not obtain any personal benefit under such action.

According to the returns made to the Royal Commissioners, the Blacksmiths' Company now comprises four keepers or wardens, twenty-one assistants, the Livery, and the yeomanry. The freedom of the Company is obtainable by servitude (as an apprentice), by patrimony, and by redemption. Formerly a quarterage of 4*s*. per annum was collected, but this caused much trouble in the collection. Females were formerly admitted, but none during the last twenty years. For thirty years previous to 1833 the admissions or calls to the Livery were often one or two only a

THE "EVIL ONE" ON HIS ROUNDS SEES THE EFFECT OF THE TREATY.

THE HORSESHOE PUTS TO FLIGHT THE DEVIL, AND PURSUES THE "EVIL ONE" AND ALL HIS EVIL COMPANIONS.

year, the highest years being 1805, 1810, and 1818, when ten, eleven, and ten respectively were admitted. During the same period the freemen numbered from six to twenty a year; in 1813 and 1818 the actual admittances were twenty-one. In 1834 about three-fifths of the Livery were, or had been, smiths, and of the whole Company nearly one-half were of the trade.

There is one advantage in this Company—the calls to the Livery go by rotation from the lists of the yeomanry, and according to seniority. In 1882 there were eighty-three freemen and eighty-one liverymen. As deaths take place a fresh "call" is made, although in the nine years ending 1879 only thirty-two were admitted freemen. Another difficulty has arisen as regards apprentices; only three were admitted in the past ten years. Persons, even freemen, have been led astray by the "know-nothings" of society, and have simply been persuaded to believe that the City apprenticeship is now of no value. We know different; and hence we heartily applaud the endeavours of the Company of Blacksmiths and their energetic clerk, Mr. W. B. Garrett, in holding the exhibition in 1889 in the Ironmongers' Hall, and promoting technical education among the rising generation of the trade, art, or mystery. The Corporation of London also proposes to make the "indenture" more conformable to the times, and this, too, is a step in the right direction.

The Blacksmiths' Company now holds its meetings at Guildhall. Formerly they met in the Blacksmiths' Hall standing on Lambeth Hill, Doctors' Commons, which in Hughson's time (1806) was "a much neglected structure," and yet "a good brick building with very convenient and stately apartments." This building formed part of the City lands of the Corporation of London, and by indenture dated in February, 1746, was granted on a forty years' lease by the City to "the Wardens, Keepers, and Society of the Mystery or Art of the Blacksmiths." It is described as situate in the parish of St. Mary Magdalene, Old Fish Street, having a frontage to Lambeth Hill of 76 feet 6 inches, and then used by the Company as their hall, &c. When the lease expired, the Blacksmiths held their meetings, as we have said, at Guildhall, and do so still.

The return made to the Commissioners of 1880 states, "The Company is not possessed of plate, pictures or furniture," but a loving cup, in private hands, of silver, was presented to the Company by Christopher Pym, upon his admission as clerk in 1665. The front of the stem that supports the bowl is occupied by a figure of Vulcan as a smith at his anvil, on which is engraved the motto of the Company, "By Hammer and Hand all Arts doe Stand." On the outside of the bowl are also engraved the Company's arms, which were confirmed by Sir William Segar, Garter, June 24, 1610.

Arms: Sa. a chev. or. between 3 hammers ar. handled of the second, ducally crowned of the last.

Crest: On a wreath a mount vert; thereon a phœnix with wings indorsed proper, firing herself with the sunbeams of the last.

The motto of the Company in ancient times was: "As God will so be it."

The Blacksmiths' is not a rich corporation, and the only charity it possesses is that founded by Edward Prestyn in June 1557. He left five houses in Fleet Lane and Old Bailey, charged with the simple trust for the bestowal of 4*s.* per annum among "the poor artists" of the Company. As a proof that the Company carry out the trust in accordance with the spirit which prompts right-minded citizens, the Blacksmiths receive a rental from these premises of 136*l.* a year, and yet pay away in charity 12*l.* per annum each to twelve poor persons of the Company, being 8*l.* more than the amount received! This would appear to be a mystery were it not explained that the Company privately purchased some other small properties, the rents from which help to keep themselves in existence, and enable them to augment the pensions of their poorer brethren.

We cannot omit to say a word or two about another society which bears the arms and the motto of the London Guilds, but is known as the Smiths' Company of Newcastle-on-Tyne. Like the Blacksmiths, the Smiths are an ancient fraternity, for its earliest ordinance is dated 1436, and among the peculiar enactments was that no Scotchman should be taken as an apprentice, or allowed to work for a member under a penalty of 40*s.*—a large sum in those days. In 1664 the branches of the trade represented on the Company were numerous, and in 1677 they were incorporated, having four wardens (one to be an anchor-smith), and twelve assistants, four of each to represent anchor-smiths, locksmiths, and farriers'-blacksmiths. Their hall adjoined the Blackfriars in Newcastle; the ground-floor room, a chapel, was the room in which homage was done by the Scottish King to the King of England. In 1824 there were seventy-seven members belonging to this Smiths' Company.

There have been many noteworthy members of the Blacksmiths' Guilds, although the custom of the City in olden time compelled the chief Magistrate to be "one of the twelve." Consequently the names of those citizens in this Company who have served the offices of Lord Mayor and sheriffs have been limited, and so far as we can learn the earliest only dates back to the end of the last century, when Thomas Baker, exactly a century ago—in 1789—was one of "the eyes of the Mayor" (as Stow quaintly describes the sheriffs), serving in the mayoralty of the celebrated William Pickett, who originated the grand improvement without Temple Bar, a full account of which will be found in the "Memorials" of that edifice published in 1869. The late Alderman James Abbiss was a Blacksmith, and one of the sheriffs in 1859, and in turn would have served as Lord Mayor had not illness compelled him to resign his gown.

We have numerous interesting references to the wills and other evidences of the Blacksmiths of old London, but want of space prevents even a summary. Two only, and these a century apart, are sufficiently curious to mention. William Reason, in 1568, left his livery-gowns to his brother and cousin, and to his apprentice William one of the vices in his shop and half of his files and tools. Industrious apprentices were thought of by their masters in those days. "And furder," continues Mr. Reason, "I bequeathe to the Company of Blackesmythes being of the lyvery that shall attende upon my bodye to the buriall for a repaste or drincking to be had and bestowed amongst them twentie shillings." The citizens of old London never expected their brethren to work for nothing, and funerals with the City Companies, especially with those who possessed halls, were of daily occurrence, as a reference to the "Diary of Henry Machyn,"

1550-1563, printed by the Camden Society in 1848, will amply prove. In 1674 William Rawlings, who requested to be buried in St. Stephen's Church, Coleman Street, and possessed much property about London, was a benefactor to the poor of Bromley and Bow, Middlesex. Joseph Thornhill, also a Blacksmith, who was buried at Hampstead, left by will in 1718 all his property adjacent to the well-known "Pindar of Wakefield," St. Pancras, and in which house he some time dwelt, in trust for the benefit of his two daughters. An account of this celebrated tavern and tea-gardens will be found at page 58 of Pinks and Wood's "History of Clerkenwell."

Finally, we can but echo the sentiments expressed in the return to the Royal Commissioners in 1880:—"The objects of the establishment of the Blacksmiths' Guild were (1) the promotion of good fellowship; (2) the protection and encouragement of the trade the name of which is borne by the Company;" and that the present Company "do all that is in their power" to attain the objects of such foundation whenever opportunity presents itself. The opportunity has been given them in A.D. 1889 to promote technical education by holding an exhibition at Ironmongers' Hall, and, as it is their first effort, so do we sincerely hope it is the forerunner of many successful ones in the future.

THE EXHIBITION.

(*Reprinted from* THE IRONMONGER, *March* 30, 1889.)

THE exhibition of articles specially applicable to the blacksmith's art has been held this week in the Ironmongers' Hall, Fenchurch Street. When a month ago (February 23) we called attention to the competition that had been opened by the Worshipful Company of Blacksmiths, we expressed a hope that, although it was their first effort, it might prove a successful one; and it is a pleasure to us to be able to chronicle that a most valuable and interesting proof has been given that on English soil there are still to be found journeymen and industrious apprentices who can turn out "by hammer and hand" some very creditable work.

Like most of the first exhibitions that have been held for the promotion of technical education, the Blacksmiths' has not been an extensive one. Only twenty-eight exhibitors sent in specimens, and only two dozen of these were competitors. But, if the quantity was small, the quality was good, and, we must say, far exceeded our expectations. Each exhibit was limited in weight to 20 lbs., so that the entire collection was easily arranged upon tables, &c., in the court-room of the Ironmongers' Company, who had willingly lent their brother-blacksmiths a most interesting apartment, which effectively added to the exhibition.

The exhibits comprised works by apprentices or youths, and works by journeymen—in the former three sections, and two prizes offered in each; in the latter three prizes. The apprentices or youths were in the respective sections not to exceed seventeen, nineteen, or twenty-one years of age, "the work to be pure hammer-work of his own production of any article of ornament or utility." The journeymen's work was to be specially "table ornamentation or panel," the three prizes being 10*l.*, 7*l.* 10*s.*, and 5*l.*, both apprentices and journeymen to have a certificate of merit in addition. The majority of the exhibitors were of the metropolis, but in a few instances the North, even as far off as Midlothian, sent competitors.

The judges met at Ironmongers' Hall on Tuesday last to inspect the exhibits, and were in several instances sorely tried, for most of the work sent in was, as we stated, very creditable. The Blacksmiths called to their aid skilled practical craftsmen outside their own body, so that the decisions arrived at must be considered eminently satisfactory. The general public viewed the exhibits on Wednesday and Thursday, and on Friday (yesterday) afternoon the prizes were awarded to the successful competitors in the fine

Hall of the Ironmongers in the presence of a numerous company. The following were the successful recipients:—

APPRENTICES AND YOUTHS.

1.—A. Harvey, 33 Marsham Street, Westminster, gas-bracket. First prize, first section, 3*l*.

2.—Arthur Beaver, 4 Victoria Terrace, Kilburn, electric table-lamp. Second prize, first section, 2*l*.

3.—J. B. Imison, 31 Rowena Crescent, Battersea, suspending-lamps. First prize, second section, 4*l*. and medal.

4.—C. Baker, 17 South Wharf Road, Paddington, three-candle bracket. Second prize, second section, 3*l*.

5.—A. W. Elwood, 9 Kennington Park Gardens, two panels, 40 × 10½. First prize, third section, 5*l*.

6.—F. Burkitt, 4 Great Suffolk Street, Southwark, three-candle stand. Second prize, third section, 4*l*. and medal.

JOURNEYMEN.

1.—J. Snailum, 66 Clarendon Road, Hornsey, panel, 36 × 13½. First prize, 10*l*.

2.—H. Ross, 13 Melton Street, N.W., bracket and oil-lamp. Second prize, 7*l*. 10*s*.

3.—T. R. Kendall, 11 Haymerle Road, Peckham, suspending-lamp holder, third prize, 5*l*.

In the preface to their list of exhibits the Company (through their energetic clerk, Mr. W. B. Garrett) appeal to exhibitors:

> The Blacksmiths' Company initiate this exhibition in the hope that British workmen will once more come to the front, and show that they can make as good and as elegant articles, both for use and ornament, as can the foreign artisan. Many persons who visited the Italian Exhibition last year saw what that country could produce, and must have been struck by the number of articles in ornamental ironwork sold, and, in many instances, in which copies were ordered. Why does not the English workman endeavour to follow—shall I not say lead?—in such work, and so retain in this country a growing and profitable industry?

We can endorse this appeal, and hope that the first exhibition may be but the forerunner of many others, each to be more successful than its predecessor.

The Blacksmiths expressed their best thanks to the Ironmongers for so kindly lending their hall, as also to Sir P. C. Owen and his staff at the South Kensington Museum for sending on loan a most interesting and valuable collection of ancient ironwork, chiefly of the fifteenth, sixteenth, and seventeenth century. Among the articles exhibited were:—

Keys of various countries.
Fire-dog (Venetian), sixteenth century.
Prow of a gondola, fifteenth century.
Knocker (Italian), fifteenth century.
Knocker (German), about 1600.
Candlesticks and snuffer-stands.
Locks, various dates.

One of the wardens of the Blacksmiths' Company, Mr. J. F Clarke, sent for exhibition several interesting articles, including a large representation of the armorial shield of the Company, whose motto is: "By Hammer and Hand all Arts do Stand."

SPOTTISWOODE, & CO., PRINTERS, NEW STREET SQUARE, LONDON, E.C.

www.ingramcontent.com/pod-product-compliance
Lightning Source LLC
Chambersburg PA
CBHW031447270326
41930CB00007B/906
9783337180935